# Intellectuals and Power

# Intellectuals and Power

## The Insurrection of the Victim

François Laruelle

in conversation with Philippe Petit

Translated by Anthony Paul Smith

polity

First published in French as *L'ultime honneur des intellectuels* © Éditions Textuel, 2003. 13 Quai de Conti -75006 Paris. www.editionstextuel.com

This English edition © Polity Press, 2015

Polity Press
65 Bridge Street
Cambridge CB2 1UR, UK

Polity Press
350 Main Street
Malden, MA 02148, USA

ISBN-13: 978-0-7456-6840-6
ISBN-13: 978-0-7456-6841-3 (pb)

A catalogue record for this book is available from the British Library.

Typeset in 11 on 14 pt Sabon by
Servis Filmsetting Ltd, Stockport, Cheshire
Printed and bound in Great Britain by T.J. International, Padstow, Cornwall

The publisher has used its best endeavors to ensure that the URLs for external websites referred to in this book are correct and active at the time of going to press. However, the publisher has no responsibility for the websites and can make no guarantee that a site will remain live or that the content is or will remain appropriate.

Every effort has been made to trace all copyright holders, but if any have been inadvertently overlooked the publisher will be pleased to include any necessary credits in any subsequent reprint or edition.

For further information on Polity, visit our website: politybooks.com

# Contents

# Translator's preface

This translation was completed a few weeks after the Boston Marathon bombing in April of 2013. Watching the predictable parade of the usual personalities who pass for intellectuals on the 24–hour news networks brought home and confirmed the basic thesis of Laruelle's critique of intellectuals in this book: intellectuals, on both the right and left, do not concern themselves with victims, but only with transcendentals that are mediatized, turned into media-friendly concepts. These include classical philosophical transcendentals like justice, truth, the rights of man or human rights, fairness, justifiable violence, etc. In each case, viewers of either the American talking-head shows, whether on liberal MSNBC or conservative FOX, or British news shows like *Newsnight* will be familiar with the way intellectuals parade themselves before the cameras, spouting off in support of some stance based upon these transcendental abstractions. I am highlighting the transcendental nature of these abstractions precisely because Laruelle's point is not to reject abstraction (though he prefers to speak of them as a singularity or "one abstract"), but to reject the transcendental illusion produced by these intellectuals before the cameras or on the op-ed pages of your daily newspaper. What Laruelle offers his readers here is a vision of intellectuals' role in the light of the critical and constructive project of non-philosophy. One that seeks to escape from the inanities of the so-called "intellectuals" whose very subsistence is guaranteed by their taking some stand on any issue whatsoever – and taking that stand on deadline! – into a higher form of thinking, one that is ultimately human and thinks from the victim rather than according to these transcendental abstractions.

In this introduction I will not detail the various hypotheses – as Laruelle describes his reflections here – that he puts forward in the course of this conversation with Philippe Petit. Petit's "Interviewer's Preface" already sets up and offers a summary of the conversation that follows. This preface will be limited to introducing Petit and highlighting how this book, originally published in France in 2003, fits within the wider project of Laruelle's non-philosophy.

Conducting the interview, as already mentioned, is Philippe Petit, who also is the general editor for the series Conversations pour demain [Conversations for Tomorrow] in which *L'ultime honneur des intellectuels* [translated here as *Intellectuals and Power*] originally appeared. This series of books consists of interviews with important public intellectuals in France including thinkers who may be familiar to Anglophone readers, like Paul Virilio and Julia Kristeva. Bringing philosophers into conversation is a certain passion of Petit as this interview with Laruelle sits among Petit's other book-length interviews with Bernard Stiegler and Jean Baudrillard.[1] In these interviews Petit brings his training as a journalist together with his training in philosophy, in which he holds the French equivalent of a doctorate. The reader will see this on display as Petit challenges Laruelle to clarify his own non-philosophical concepts in the light of other philosophers' ideas, and as he challenges Laruelle to make those concepts speak in the light of current events.

*Intellectuals and Power* follows on from themes begun in Laruelle's *Ethique de l'Étranger* (2000) and his *Future Christ: A Lesson in Heresy* (2002/2010). Both of these texts touch on major issues in philosophical ethics, namely the lived reality of victims of crimes against humanity, the historical instance of the Shoah, as well as the problems of memory inherent in these sorts of massively destructive events. However, it is here in *Intellectuals and Power* that the problematic of victims emerges for the first time in Laruelle's work. This is given its most sustained treatment in his *General Theory of Victims*, forthcoming with Polity in a translation by Jessie Hock and Alex Dubilet (original French edition published in 2012). But it is here that the theme of victims emerges in explicit reference to those who claim to be able to speak for them – the intellectuals – and whose failure to truly think from the victim, rather than simply about her, is revealed by Laruelle.

Non-Philosophy has always been concerned with the ethical and the political, with Laruelle's earliest works

---

[1] Bernard Stiegler, *Economie de l'hypermatériel et psychopouvoir: Entretiens avec Philippe Petit et Vincent Bontems* (Paris: Mille et une nuits, 2008), and Jean Baudrillard, *Paroxysm*, trans. Chris Turner (London: Verso, 1998).

(all of which remain untranslated at the time of this publication) explicitly developing concepts related to the political thematics of revolution, power, and the status of minorities. However, there is a marked difference between Laruelle's engagement with ethics and politics and those of his contemporary Alain Badiou, who is a constant reference point in this interview. That difference is simply that Laruelle refuses to separate ethics and politics as Badiou insists upon doing. Laruelle discusses this difference here, but it reaches its fullest expression in his *Anti-Badiou* (translated into English by Robin Mackey for Bloomsbury). What Laruelle objects to in this separation is the way it serves to underline the supremacy of philosophy over the human, of saying that, in some sense, one should subject oneself to the master of politics instead of the master of ethics. For Laruelle, neither ethics nor politics should master the human, but rather both are simply material or tools for the human to use in the construction of a truly human or humane utopia. Thus his concern with politics has always sought to avoid the usual form of politics, always determined by whether it fits into a media-friendly narrative or already-existing politics which are recognizably liberal, leftist, or right-wing. While Laruelle is clearly aligned on the Left of the political spectrum, as can be seen in his emphasis on Marxism and a recognition that human beings require to have their means of subsistence safeguarded regardless of anything else, he is not satisfied with the scripted dialog of politics.

However, breaking that scripted dialog by demanding that intellectuals, philosophers, and theorists of all kinds turn to the victim is not some fetishization of victims that would turn them into a transcendent term that stops all conversation. But it is a recognition that these intellectuals and philosophy almost always turn away from the victim. The victim-in-person, as Laruelle calls her to highlight her real character, her lived or flesh-and-blood character, does not inspire philosophers and intellectuals in the same way that heroes, or brave resisters, or those who turn the tide and heroically vanquish their enemies, do. So, the victim becomes the unthought of philosophy, a stumbling block to its standard practice. She must then become a presupposed for any attempt to think ethics and politics anew, in defense of the human.

There are a number of choices I have made in the course of translating this text that should be highlighted here so that the reader can keep them in mind. In general, there are inherent difficulties in translating Laruelle's work that go to the heart of his theoretical practice. Laruelle has highlighted in many of his publications the importance of non-philosophical syntax in combating the standard syntax of philosophy. This means that the way he writes in French is often experimental, with a certain disregard for ease of reading. In order to capture this syntax, I always tend toward a more literal translation of his works. At times I have aimed for a freer translation, but in general I prefer the way in which a literal translation causes the reader to slow down in the same way a reader is suddenly slowed by Laruelle's French prose.

Throughout his work Laruelle uses the past participle of verbs in a technical way. For example, *v*écu is the past participle of *vivre*, meaning to live, but is normally translated in philosophical texts as "lived experience."

As the meaning of Laruelle's usage is to highlight the actual, radically immanent sense of some action, then translating it in this way, though in some sense more idiomatic, would cover over that technical meaning as it suggests a distance between what is lived and the experience of it. Distance for Laruelle is always the expression of some form of transcendence and so would be contrary to the intended meaning. In those cases where the usage struck me as important, I have translated *vécu* as "lived."

Along the same lines of attempting to express something as radical immanence, Laruelle explicitly distinguishes between *un présupposé*, which could be translated as "presupposition" for a more idiomatic rendering, and *présupposition philosophique* or "philosophical presupposition." I have rendered *un présupposé* as "a presupposed" / "one presupposed" to highlight this difference. The same follows when Laruelle distinguishes between "an abstract" / "one abstract" and an abstraction.

Laruelle often uses formulations such as the prefix "auto," i.e. "auto-affection." Often, these uses of "auto" could be translated as "self" as in "self-defense." However, after a discussion with the author, I have rendered many of these using "auto" to highlight the particular character of radical immanence that Laruelle wants to emphasize and to avoid the potentially confusing philosophical baggage of the "self" implied in the usual formulations. In this way, I have followed the translators of Michel Henry's work, which also serves to highlight the great influence Henry's work has had on Laruelle.

*Médiatique* is another major adjectival term that

recurs throughout the text but resists easy translation. In general the term is used in the text to refer to ideas or figures that we might call "camera-ready" or "media-friendly." That is, they can fit into already-constructed media narratives or are suitable for easy consumption by being translated into sound bites. Sometimes in the text such a translation did not seem to fit and so I have sometimes rendered it with the neologism "mediatized" to suggest the rendering of the noun into something media-friendly or amenable to being expressed through media.

Laruelle uses terminology in the book that has been introduced in earlier works of his and so does not attempt to explain them for the reader. Chief among them is his use of "Man-in-person" or his strange use of brackets and hyphens. In general these formulations are not as mystifying as readers may first assume. For example, "Man-in-person" and variants of this phrase refer to the usual sense of "in person" we also have in English, where someone is there in all actuality. The sense Laruelle is putting across here is that there is no separation between the idea and the concrete reality, as there exists in abstractions concerning what a human being is – like "a political animal" and so on. I direct readers to the translators' prefaces of *Future Christ* and *Principles of Non-Philosophy* for further explications of this vocabulary and syntax, as well as to A. P. Smith, *Laruelle: A Stranger Thought* (Polity, forthcoming).

Laruelle's use of "Man" throughout the text always refers to the generic-being or species-being of human beings. Of course this opens up Laruelle to charges that his non-philosophy is, like that of the majority of philosophers, a male-oriented philosophy. In works that have followed *Intellectuals and Power*, Laruelle has attempted to correct this by referring to the "Human-in-person" precisely because he is trying to think the human in his or her radical immanence and so beyond sexual difference, but without slipping into the usual mistake of confusing a particular (a biological male human being) with the universal. In attempting to high-light this later attempt without overstepping my rights as a translator, I have availed myself of an opportunity coded into the gendered nature of French as a Romance language. As readers likely know, all nouns and their adjectives are either masculine or feminine. Thus, "intel-lectual" in French is masculine and "victim" is feminine. I have then referred to intellectuals with the general pronoun "he" (though this does not of course mean that there are no women intellectuals), and victims with the pronoun "she" (though this does not mean that there are no men who are victims). This aligning of women and victims is not meant to suggest a weakness on the part of women, especially since Laruelle's point that philosophers have never really dealt with the victim in some ways parallels Irigaray when she says that phi-losophy has not truly thought from the perspective of a woman.[2]

Finally, Laruelle marks a difference between what he terms dominant intellectuals, who carry various adjec-tives like engaged, humanitarian, right-wing, left-wing, etc., and what he terms the determined intellectual. A

---

[2] Those interested in a discussion of how Laruelle's non-philosophy may in-teract with gender theory and feminist philosophy should look to Katerina Kolozova's *Cut of the Real: Subjectivity and Poststructuralist Philosophy* (New York: Columbia University Press, 2014), as well as the preface to Kolozova's book written by Laruelle.

reader going too quickly might confuse this with an intellectual who is particularly dedicated to some task, but the adjective expresses a theoretical point Laruelle is making. The determined intellectual is an intellectual whose character is determined in the sense of conditioned or driven by his or her relationship to the victim. Laruelle's understanding of determination owes much to his study of Marx, who in turn was influenced in his thinking by Hegel, and so readers should bear in mind the Hegelian meaning of "determined" as found in the master–slave dialectic when coming across this term.

# *Interviewer's preface*

An inflexible rigor and a certain easing of the conditions of thought: the double injunction animating the work of François Laruelle will surprise more than one reader. Attracted by the title, *Intellectuals and Power*, intrigued by the back cover, the neophyte, in total innocence, will get to know the author of *Une biographie de l'homme ordinaire* (1985) and *Future Christ: A Lesson in Heresy* (2002 and 2010 in English translation). In doing so, the reader may be surprised by the theoretical audacity of someone who began his career right off the bat as a heretic nearly 20 years ago, composing little blue notebooks that were stapled together with care, overseeing their selling and distribution himself.

This reader will be surprised by the relentless dialogue – maybe puzzled, or even annoyed, by it – but he doesn't know how lucky he is. Whether he resists agreeing to the author's "spiritual" thought, to his "unlearned" (and untaught) knowing; whether he lets himself be taken by his affirmation of a radical humanity, one that is primitive as much as future; whether he adheres or not to his peacemaking intentions – either way he cannot escape Laruelle's force of conviction or do anything but admire his uncompromising approach. The reader of this conversation may balk, finding the tone high and mighty, the responses unnerving, but he will have no choice, we believe, but to salute the performance of one of our greatest contemporary thinkers. The reader will undoubtedly be astonished by his audacity, by his fierce will to disrupt the most common uses of philosophy, but also the most authoritarian and sophisticated ones. He will be captivated, unwillingly, as we can be by a shameful secret, by an interior experience that is without remainder, mute, and inaudible to whatever transcendence there may be.

For once, and perhaps for the first time, if the reader has never heard "non-philosophy" discussed, he will not be *on the road*,[1] enlisted amidst the noise and fury of current events, of History, of dominant discourses, be they the discourses of resistance to barbarism or hardship, those of grievance or the intolerable, or those of the hopes of little girls and the courage of heroes.[2] He will not be required to stand before the gates of Hell or set off on the path to infinity. He will not be obliged to choose one philosophy from amongst others and to determine himself according to what is written or said in the marketplace of ideas. Whether the reader gives his consent to some philosophy or wonders about the way in which the subject is caused by the thought of the Other, these are, for Laruelle, equivalent motives as

---

[1] English in original. [Translator's note.]
[2] An oblique reference to Charles Péguy's poem "La petite fille espérance." [Translator's note.]

soon as we make them dependent upon the "Principle of Sufficient Philosophy" according to which everything would be philosophizable. The reader will thus have the pleasure of testing this principle of mastery and of then confronting it. He will have the opportunity to explore it practically through a case study: the role of the intellectuals. He will experience a new regime of thought, a change in paradigm concerning what the function of intellectuals is today in their relationship to victims and to current events generally. Facing philosophy which is always judge or plaintiff, which is always a self-including thought, facing what presses the intellectuals to act, what impels them to join the fray, or to retire to their backyard, the author of the *Principe de minorité* (1981) offers them an exit by going "higher up" [*par le haut*]. He means to liberate intellectuals from their reciprocal ascendency and resituate them within the fundamental philosophical presuppositions that drive them. But he does this so as to find a better way to escape the traps of philosophy and, by doing so, avoids simply reproducing the coercion of this situation. Laruelle means to care for History and even Time, breaking the circle of vengeance, transforming thought, and enabling it to present its potential aid to and according to the victims rather than redoubling their unhappiness by chaining them to their condition as victims. He no longer wants to lock them in a revolving door of crime and its reparation, living in a state of permanent self-defense. He refuses to fight misfortune in the name of abstract values, such as justice or truth, which treat their "real" content with disdain, that content of "Man-in-person" and here even "Victim-in-person." He attempts to think the Victim as distinct and separate from the philosophical circle.

He describes what would be a new cause for man, a new destination for the intellectual, in a world submitted to the laws of the philosophically thinkable (world, history, and thought) . . .

The author, we shall see, does not pretend to contribute to the ongoing debates about the new reactionaries, the end of intellectuals, the silence of scholars, their engagement within society, or other considerations about the good fortunes and misfortunes of those men, for example, who took part in the Grand Refusal during the Dreyfus Affair. He does not try to substitute one belief for another, but to explain belief in the world as it is given. He seeks to explain why history is stuck, slips, repeats itself, and why humanist protest redoubles its excesses. He offers us a new face of dignity. A new way of entering into the future, of acting otherwise, of being determined by the Real and not wearing ourselves down trying to determine it. This is by far the most difficult operation to grasp in the thought of Laruelle; it is also the one most contested by philosophers, and yet it is the most essential one for understanding the author. Because, whether one is or is not a philosopher, it is hardly possible to escape philosophical belief – unless, that is, we seriously practice an anti-philosophy.

It is difficult, outside of psychoanalysis and the arts, or even science, to avoid being plunged into this metaphysical ocean, an ocean without shore or bearings, of which Kant spoke. We are all philosophers – mostly, for that matter, without realizing it – because we have to be fair to the creators of concepts and to courageous minds. But François Laruelle's path is different. The courage that he comes to have no longer obeys the laws of transcendence. He does not espouse philosophy's sufficiency, philosophy's will to believe it is able to think the Real such as it is, "whereas philosophy thinks it only as it is, as such." He breaks "the idea of the mirror, of reflection, of a double in the identical." He renounces metaphysical *hubris*, all by embracing the treatment of philosophy's declarations [énoncés] as materials open to being worked upon. He fashions clones from philosophical and analytic declarations. Through ascesis and collective action, he prepares the attack of the clones. Following the example of Kleist, he does not ask us to give him "air, air!" and does not despairingly search for possibilities, for lines of flight, for new bifurcations, for new adventures – there is capitalism and universal history for that – he fastens himself to a new cause, a new way of thinking the Victim, from the ground of immanence, so as to "do otherwise." Of course, he works with the World, but without reproducing it, and without dramatizing it. He comes down from the heights of transcendence once and for all.

It is not at all surprising that an author who draws concurrently upon so many marginal people, formed in the school of Nietzsche, Heidegger, Derrida, and Deleuze, a lover of poetry and touched very early on by art, as seen in his first work on Félix Ravaisson (1971), has invented in solitude a new discipline with a prophetic name: non-philosophy. Laruelle has never really had a master, but he has crossed paths and debated with nearly all his contemporaries, including the debate with the former Minister of National Education, Luc Ferry, in a memorable edition of *La Décision philosophique* that appeared in 1989. He started with philosophy as a quasi-autodidact and practiced it up to the point of overdose, of suffocation. But not in order to raise up a new philosophy. Indeed, his ambition, from the mid-1980s, was to break – not without loss or drama – with this queen of the sciences and her appearances. The founder of non-philosophy followed his work with an unfailing perseverance. In solitude, at first, with his "Pourquoi pas la philosophie?" journals – no one knew at the time whether these were inspired by Péguy or by the Samizdat literature of the Eastern European dissidents. Then in collective recognition, since non-philosophy, as savage as it was, and despite the innumerable forms of institutional resistance, has since given rise to several collectives, to works and websites, to the Organisation non-philosophique internationale (ONPHI).[3]

And what perseverance in thinking according to the Real, in positing the Real as not determinable by thought! What a strange Real it is in which thought is given or determined according to its own mode, and not the Real according to the mode of thought! An unheard-of presupposition, which "clones" thought, and allows the author to settle into a strictly human future, like Bergson said about settling into duration, without which the future falls into the to-come that philosophy traces for itself. What a peculiar man Laruelle's Man-in-person is, because he is not an absolute starting point, nor an enlarged *cogito*, but a radical starting point, a "given-without-givenness," which evades phenomenology as much as it evades the philosophies of difference that Laruelle has analyzed and dismantled like no one else. This Man, who is ourselves, does not exist as we exist in the World; this Man is not representable on a background of appearance–disappearance, of absence–

[3] www.onphi.org.

presence; this Man is not announced as some power of being within the chaos of multiplicities – but this Man consists, outside of all worldly consistency, as one who imposes himself on thought. "He is truly spiritual, quite possibly without spirit, who knows himself to be such in a totally different way (in an unlearned way), different from the way that consciousness knows of itself" writes Laruelle in one of his numerous lectures. This is not the place to describe this lived discipline of immanence, nor to summarize Laruelle's transcendental method. Some young followers have already seen to that.[4] But it is important to make the reader appreciate that Laruelle is an original and methodological spiritual type and not a "spiritualist!" It wasn't on a sudden impulse that Laruelle decided to suspend the assumed legislative authority that philosophy proclaims over the Real. It was not just some appetite for destruction that led him to take up the task of non-philosophy. One does not destroy Parmenides, but only attacks the arrogance [*suffisance*] of Parmenides. Cartesian, Kantian, then Bergsonian and Deleuzian; a longstanding Platonist, admirer of Levinas and Michel Henry, before embarking on his own path; he was, and still is, all that at once. But

---

[4] *Initiation à la pensée de François Laruelle,* by Juan Diego Blanco, preceded by *Qu'est-ce que la non-philosophy?* by François Laruelle (Paris: L'Harmattan, 1997), *La Non-Philosophie de François Laruelle* by Hughes Choplin (Paris: Kimé, 2000), *Deleuze et Laruelle* by Erik del Bufalo (Paris: Kimé, 2002). [English readers may want to consult *Laruelle and Non-Philosophy,* edited by John Maoilearca and Anthony Paul Smith (Edinburgh: Edinburgh University Press, 2012); Anthony Paul Smith, *Laruelle: A Stranger Thought* (Cambridge: Polity, forthcoming); Alexander R. Galloway, *Laruelle: Against the Digital* (Minneapolis: University of Minnesota Press, 2014); and John Ó Maoilearca, *Postural Mutations: Laruelle and Nonhuman Philosophy* (Minneapolis: University of Minnesota Press, 2014).] [Translators note.]

he was lacking a principle: an omega point that would prove to him that philosophy was going round in circles, just as, in this book, dominant intellectuals go round in circles, sometimes lashing out in the arena, sometimes beating a retreat, being for or against war, always ready to take on the mantel of responsibility, always inclined to grab hold of distant causes, and to believe in their impact. "That's the opium of the intellectual and it is the opium of philosophy, though it only really acts in an oblique way" protests Laruelle, who writes about himself that he was a "junkie for Being."

By what right? From his point of entry, which is a true point of departure that we will not talk about as if Laruelle found it like a revelation, an illumination – rather it is what he has discovered gradually over the course of a long – a very long – research program that from the beginning has been related to the forgetting of the One. From a discovery tested in a method, previously "trans-valued" and generalized, since the immanence of the One would subsequently become the Real and then the "Name-of-Man." And he will supply the key to understanding the "Principle of Sufficient Philosophy," this infinite philosophizability, which governs, according to Laruelle, the function of the dominant intellectuals and their relation to current affairs and to their urgency, incapable of resisting the World except in a relationship of non-conformity that would have to be invented with that World. The eternal treason of the intellectuals . . .

This is the journey condensed in this conversation, whose consequences are brought out in the genealogy of intellectuals that is on display here. Neither an anti-conformist intellectual, nor a disengaged intellectual, nor a heroic philosopher, not even a media-friendly intellectual, specific, humanitarian, or whatever you like! The new function of the intellectuals described in this *Intellectuals and Power* is not indebted to any of these attributes. The "determined intellectual" (determined by the Name-of-Man), defended forcefully by Laruelle, completely shatters the order of the dialectic, so often experienced biasedly and as the dominant opinion. He opens the windows to thought and authorizes new practices. He introduces the reader to a kind of utopia never seen before. "I assume the worst, but under a human condition," writes Laruelle, "so as not to sink into the worst of the worst."

To those who defend themselves from the World and its gregariousness by becoming dancing artists or nimble spirits, to those who protect themselves from the unhappiness of men by officially taking responsibility for immediately reacting to distressing situations, to all those who struggle to protect themselves from adversity or mediocrity, François Laruelle, we say, offers them an exit upwards. The image falls in on itself. Because we will not find in this book any "exit," nor any "end." Only protection and a defense against the subjugation of humankind. We will find a "spirit of struggle" unconditioned by the natural belief in history, and so a damn fine [*sacré*] lesson in heresy.[5]

Philippe Petit

[5] The French word *sacré* has the odd function of being both the word for "sacred" and a mild cuss-word akin to "damn" in English. The play on the double meaning of the word is lost here, but is worth flagging up. [Translator's note.]

# Prologue

Philippe Petit (PP): *From Raymond Aron's* The Opium of the Intellectuals *(1955; English translation 1957) to Jean-Paul Sartre's* Plaidoyer pour les intellectuels *(1972)* [A Defense of the Intellectuals], *Jean-François Lyotard's* Tombeau de l'intellectuel et autres papiers *(1984)* [Tombstone for the Intellectual and Other Papers], *and Régis Debray's* I.F. suite et fin *(2000)* [The Last and Final French Intellectual], *alongside still more works, there has not been a decade in which we have not seen French thinkers interrogating the role and function of intellectuals in society. We regularly witness a confrontation between them, or even intellectuals putting other intellectuals to death. After the men of the Grand Refusal – the French intellectuals of the Dreyfus Affair – came the men without a mandate, as Sartre put it. After him, an interminable crowd of adjectives has gathered to glorify the very name of the intellectual: engaged, specific, media-friendly, radical, humanitarian, etc. Now, there is you, if I dare say it, you, the solitary thinker, the inventor of a new discipline: non-philosophy – the founder of a new school despite himself – so there you are, keen to re-gild the role or function of the intellectuals, to save the honor of the intellectuals, to remove them from their internecine wars, to give them the means to avoid having to heap unhappiness on top of unhappiness, making them capable of resisting the pressures of the World and History! I will stop myself, because we don't want to open this dialog without presenting some precautions and considerations for the reader who has not yet had the chance to get to know you. Why intervene in the question of intellectuals? What is it that pushes you to go there? What does it mean in your work to declare the question of the intellectuals' survival to be an open question?*

François Laruelle (FL): The honor of the intellectuals? That's saying a lot ... I am not a "personality" [*signature*] and I am not qualified to pass judgment on anyone who does a job that I do not do myself. On the other hand, the ultimate honor, the last chance [*ultime honneur*], yes. Without asking for anyone's authorization, though I don't derive authorization from myself either. It is an ultimatum, no less, addressed to them, though I would find it really hard to honor their failure to respond to such an ultimatum by declaring war upon them. This is only an extension of prospective paths opened up by my *Ethique de l'Étranger* as well as by *Future Christ*, and as such it is a declaration of peace.

PP: *An end of intellectuals? A death of intellectuals? Apparently you aren't satisfied by the thematic of the disappearance of intellectuals. You are concerned with the suspension of war between intellectuals. Is it possi-*

*ble to be done with that war? Can you clarify from the outset your diagnostic on the role of intellectuals?*

FR: I would like less to pass judgment than to express a certain reaction of incredulity about the way in which they fulfil their function. They are a cross for philosophy, I do indeed say "Philosophy with a capital P" [*la philosophie*], being one of the few that believes philosophy possesses an identity and consistency beyond the systems of "metaphysics" or "logocentrism." In the current situation, some are of course more and more indefensible, marked by a certain ambitiousness, a certain opportunism, and a certain reactionary spirit. Maybe this image will come to contrast quite violently with the great classical intellectuals, Voltaire and the Enlightenment philosophers, Sartre and the so-called "left intellectuals" of the 1950s. They were obsessed with justice and with causes, making history with the defense of those causes. The image of the intellectual has become blurrier, even though there have always been many right-wing intellectuals – one should never forget that. But we have reached a new low, a philosophical degree close to zero in the works of the most boisterous amongst them. Can a cynical and complicit society lead to anything else? I wonder if, more broadly, the intellectual is not a more or less direct descendant of the ancient sophist – in any case, I will try to take up this problem in the lineage of Plato, situating the intellectual between the sophist, to whom he is related, and the philosopher. I will first place the intellectuals on a philosophical horizon that I will assume to be invariant in its structure, and, second, place them in a totally different element, not a metaphilosophical one, but one I call non-philosophical, which I will progressively explain using precisely the example of the intellectual. So, first a typological and structural perspective, replacing – as it is philosophically more radical – the histories or sociologies of intellectuals which are so very French and somewhat revisionist. Then, a new discipline – the equivalent of a psychoanalysis adapted to the intellectual type and his special theoretical conditions.

PP: *Why do you say that intellectuals today can only be complicit? You generalize the situation. But on certain questions – the veil in schools, education, cloning – we can't talk about complicity, can we?*

FL: Complicity is not just the rule that brings out notable exceptions, of course – it is also more than the rule, it is the principle of every philosophical vision of the World. And so the exceptions are worth just as much as they usually are . . . In any event, complicity is love of the generalized exception. That has been established for a long time.

PP: *So what disturbs you then is the commentary on current events, the indissoluble connection that unites intellectuals with history?*

FL: This indissolubleness is like the passion for complicity; it is the same problem and has the same solution. Yes, current events, not necessarily contemporary, but current events are a real problem that binds intellectuals hand and foot to history, politics, even to religion, to the "demands of the present" outside of which they feel like they don't exist [*inexistants*] and lack purpose. Why not say it, there is a real delirium for and a real cowardliness in all-

---

responsibility.[1] I try to decouple them from the abstract and anonymous values in the name of which they paradoxically attach themselves to current events: whether it concerns soil, blood, race, the earth, filiations, human rights, or even class struggle. I decouple so as to better recouple them with another object, one which the intellectuals sometimes invoke or pay tribute to but which, in my view, they do not appreciate in its discrete, its pitiless insistence – the human victim. It isn't clear that the victims call for this kind of responsibility or are satisfied with it. So the concern here is with re-associating the intellectual with his genuine object, which has that property of not quite becoming a part of history. The task is securing that change of function to this new cause that determines its destination. What would an intellectual be if his object was no longer justice or truth as abstract values, but only the Victim as the "real" content of these values?

PP: *Does this Victim have something to do with current events? If it is necessary to re-associate the intellectual with his genuine object, then what about the objects of past intellectuals?*

FL: I believe that the first operation to undertake is a philosophical re-contextualization of the intellectual. Putting the intellectual back in his true scene requires first of all putting him back in the invariant horizon of philosophy. Of course, intellectuals are often professional philosophers or people who manipulate

---

[1] This is another formula common to Laruelle's work, adding *tout* to a noun. After discussions with the author regarding the precise meaning, I have rendered this as "all-X," meaning that the noun is uniquely what it is, excluding all relations and all other predicates. [Translator's note.]

philosophy, who know how to skilfully use philosophy to dazzle those who are not philosophers. But I want to discuss something altogether different: there is a genealogy of the function of the intellectual internal to philosophy itself. At best, we have understood the function of the intellectual from the perspective of vast regions of experience like theology, politics, moral theory, law, literature, without placing this experience again in its ultimate and universal context, its philosophical possibility. From this specific point of view, I cannot make out any difference between left-wing intellectuals and right-wing intellectuals, however unfair this apparent indifference is. In so far as they are linked to philosophy, and philosophy has the potential to be either more to the right or more to the left according to empirical or local historical determinations, this difference is secondary for the time being. It seems to me important to attempt a kind of reinsertion of the intellectual into his natural environment and to understand what kind of use he makes of philosophy.

PP: *How is this genealogy you evoke established? How does one deal with the lines of relation and family that distinguish the intellectuals from one another? Michel Foucault said, "For a long period the left intellectual spoke and his right to speak in the capacity of master of truth and justice was acknowledged. He was heard or purported to make himself heard, as the spokesman of the universal. To be an intellectual meant something like being the consciousness/conscience of us all."*[2] *This*

---

[2] Michel Foucault, *Knowledge/Power: Selected Interviews & Other Writings 1972–1977*, edited by Colin Gorden (New York: Pantheon Books, 1977), p. 126. [Translation slightly modified.]

*conscience, to say the least, has been shaken. Alain Finkielkraut, for example, might be considered to be a European intellectual, but what do we call Alain Badiou when he makes his interventions concerning the Iraq war or the 2002 French Presidential election – do we call him an intellectual or a philosopher? Can we clearly distinguish a liberal intellectual like Pierre Manent and a "leftist" intellectual like Zaki Laïdi or Daniel Bensaïd? Are you interested in this kind of pinpointing of a specific locale amongst diverse intellectual families?*

FL: It is interesting but it doesn't interest me. I am going to let you down but not surprise you: I have no desire to begin an overview and judgement of contemporary intellectuals, putting forward names, some that are not very highly recommended and others that are highly recommended because of their intellectual rigour. Beside the professional intellectuals, that classic sociological and psychological type, there increasingly are others who can fulfil an intellectual function, meaning everyone: military men, gardeners, politicians, actors, and above all philosophers. Of course, Alain Badiou can fulfil this intellectual function, but he does not fulfil it always and everywhere. He is first a philosopher, and even a philosopher in the grand tradition. What is interesting is precisely no longer dividing up or classifying intellectuals according to domains of empirical values, to which they are linked – but to make out what constitutes, little by little, historically, on a philosophical basis, a true *intellectual function*. This function can be fulfilled by this or that individual, according to the situation, according to the possibility of some given intervention in certain conflicts and crises, according to the profession, according to political choices, according largely to the filtered mediatization of the news. But this function is more universal than those individuals who are able to take it on. There are now intellectual agents, specialized workers, middle managers, permanent workers, and temporary ones. The temporary intellectuals still are not unionized, but just wait . . .

PP: *Because you want to save this intellectual function, you have not begun with the logic of those who announce the end of intellectuals. You intend to keep both the name and the thought that surrounds it.*

FL: Indeed, because I believe that it is initially necessary, beyond the deaths, the tombs, the ends of intellectuals. And by going through these apocalypses we see that there is a function which opens up more and more, which is transformed, but remains, in a certain way, an invariant that has some necessity within philosophical structure. We have to not allow ourselves to be fascinated or impressed by stories about the intellectuals, by their war, their multiple betrayals, their current conflict. Not even – and I will return to this – by the supposed impact of their action and the necessity of their intervention. What we could call the action of the intellectuals is a structured set of practices which are not expressly the practices of philosophy or the human sciences, but which deploy such elements for a different effectual regime.[3] But this is only the start of the operation.

---

[3] *Sciences humaines* refers to a set of intellectual and academic disciplines that are roughly analogous to those which are referred to in the UK and US as the humanities and social sciences. [Translator's note.]

PP: *Don't allow yourself to be impressed! But you surely don't want to contest certain lines of descent? The Liberals, Neo-Marxists, Spinozists, whatever, are not in the same boat. Does this empirical history have any meaning?*

FL: These doctrinal or ideological kinds of identitarian claims are all well and good. But what interests me is not the meaning of their action but its cause. I do not confuse the ultimate cause of the intellectuals with the meaning that they proclaim and their historical turpitude. Besides, I refuse to exaggerate the effect of their action as they promote it. They are the victims of an appearance and a belief. Which ones? Their action is only indirect, in a roundabout way or through a certain bunching up together. It's part of the current climate [*dans l'air du temps*], but they act as if their action was direct, straight from the historic situation or the event in person. The reality of their engagement is one of being an *engagement-between* (between them) and, after that, nothing more. This belief in their impact is the opium of the intellectuals and it is the opium of philosophy, though it only really acts in an oblique way. That said, I would be the first to shoot up philosophy. We, philosophers, are we not the junkies of Being, the drug addicts of metaphysics, servants to a Logos god, lovers of all drunkenness?

PP: *Should we infer from your remarks that it is no longer necessary to take into account the engagement of intellectuals? Should we distrust their point of view on history or current events? Do we take a position immediately, for example, within a philosophical discussion*

*about war, like the one proposed by Michael Walzer
in his book on just war? Is the subjection of the intellectual to historical causes of the moment immediately
undifferentiated, or even refused?*

FL: Refused, no. Undifferentiated [*Indifférencié*], without a doubt – but provided that we have a good
understanding of the meaning of this indifference
[*indifférence*]. It does not signify a refusal or sidelin-
ing, just setting these beliefs and appearances between
parentheses, beliefs and appearances that are the fabric
covering history, but this is a suspension which implies
a new kind of relationship to what will be undifferentiated. It is not a question of disengaging absolutely, in
some quietist way. There is an infinite amount of subject matter for intellectual debates and it can only be
increased. I would gladly campaign for a *non-engaged*
intellectual if the "non-" was correctly understood as
the non- of "non-Euclidean," as a generalizing or generalized "non-" and not as a "no" of refusal. Between the
intellectual who is engaged in the classical, and above all
in the Marxist, manner, and the disengaged intellectual,
fairly realist and conformist, who opposes the engaged
intellectuals, there is another I would like to call the
non-engaged intellectual, the "non-" signifying that his
engagement is determined by a cause which itself is not
engaged, a cause which belongs neither to history nor to
society, but which makes it possible to carry on a certain
emancipatory or liberatory relation to history and to
society (in reality to philosophy and to the State reunited
as a thought-world, but I do not want to extrapolate on
that right now). So, it isn't a question of the death of the
intellectuals. Even empirically, this question of death

makes no sense. There will always be intellectuals and, above all, always philosophers to announce their death or suicide. The true problem is that of their transformation rather than their annihilation; the true problem is that of their destination, which I call "utopian."

PP: *What does a cause which isn't historical, which doesn't belong to history, signify?*

FL: Very well, a Lacanian mediation. If the intellectual himself deals with history, then the cause of the intellectual is the impossible in history, but this is an impossible which determines history and isn't content with being an "impossible child." This impossible is what I in general call "Man-in-person" or "Name-of-Man," but here under the auspices of history, I will call it Victim-in-person. This is, and isn't quite, the "absent cause."

PP: *Let's accept this: the intellectual does not belong [tombe] to history, but he happens to fall [tomber] on the battlefield. Heroes are those who came to give society its absent cause. They come to give a kind of provisional salvation, a sort of possibility that society can no longer offer. Would you be able to say something about heroes?*

FL: On the mediatized battlefield, that's for sure. He may also fall on the battlefield of history, but Péguy, for example, didn't fall because he was an intellectual. He was a solider like everyone else, cannon fodder like anyone, a victim, human and anonymous at the same time. That said, I am not torn between the hero and the victim. The classical intellectual claims to give precisely the absent cause once again. No, the absent cause doesn't need to be given within history, it is history that rather has to be given and to come out of the absent cause. The philosophers have always proclaimed themselves heroes, of virtue, of wisdom, of thought, of *physis*, philosophical heroism blooms forth in Nietzsche, there is a remainder of heroism in Heidegger, and a declared heroism in Badiou. I am not very good at putting up with philosophical heroism and all that it conceals. What I call non-philosophy, as well as what I call the victim, is not marked by heroism. Non-Philosophy is militant, not in the least because its cause, the Victim-in-person, is at bottom the definitively defeated of history. It would nevertheless be necessary to reflect on what it means to "stand up for victims" [*prendre la défense des victimes*] and not to content oneself with the usual glitz. The cradle for intellectuals is philosophy as a vision of the world that belongs to the victors, their way of deciding that history has some meaning or another, and manipulating it. I will contrast the heroic intellectual and the determined (rather than dominant) intellectual, one who can act in utter mediatized destitution . . .

PP: *Would you not say the same thing as the Resistance philosopher Jean Cavaillès?*

FL: An example, an *a posteriori* one above all, though there are others, proves nothing except its own existence. We cannot know *a priori* what an individual will do in a war, we just have some presumptions. That being said, there is a difference between a philosopher and an "intellectual," but in how they act there is a wholly other difference between these two and the witness of the

Victim-in-person. As far as communication is concerned, it is certainly there between the most abstract thought (mathematical in Cavaillès or ontological in Heidegger) and the position of the civilian and citizen. Heidegger has finally given us a very bad example of what philosophy can lead to, or what it can tolerate; Cavaillès has given us a completely different example ... But their difference in destiny is not at stake here. I suspect philosophers have a secret love for politics and in particular adore the job of counseling the prince, regardless of who the prince is anyway. They are fascinated by the force which carries on regardless, it's their force, except that theirs turns back on itself in order to limit itself; this is the bad conscience that contains the shame of half-solutions and of not going all the way. I believe that we always do philosophy in place of something that we have not been able to realize. This is its problem, which arises from regret regarding some repression or fantasy lived out as unrealizable. The philosophers are secretly seduced by power. It happened to Heidegger through the legislative, founding, and "revolutionary" aspects of Nazism, but the true example is Nietzsche, exactly because he was not especially a counselor to the prince, an inadequate function for "great politics," but he is the one who dared to place the excess or abuse of power at the heart of power. Nietzsche is the philosopher who let the cat out of the bag; he said what all the others were hiding and showed that philosophy is a permanent encroachment on the Real and can appear, or be given, in the shape of a political project. This is clearly thematized in Nietzsche: a force can only encroach on another force in order to dominate it. This is an abuse of power over knowledge or knowledge as an abuse of power – all

Foucault's orchestration. But it's already very visible in its Greek origins: philosophical transcendence contains something like *hubris,* something excessive; this is that gesture of overcoming that still lives in the intellectuals who intervene in public debates and try to transcend those debates. In this gesture of transcendence, we redis-cover the excess that is fundamentally at the root of philosophy.

PP: *Let's pick up this important aspect of the relation-ship of philosophers to concrete politics again. Today, if we paint the landscape in broad strokes, on the one side we have the followers of moral and political phi-losophy, those who, from Monique Canto-Sperber to Jürgen Habermas, situate themselves within the field of institutional politics and are some new breed of coun-selors, mediators, couriers of providential democracy or of liberal socialism. And on the other side, we have more radical philosophers whom we find on the margins of official parties. How do you see this new bipartition between those who situate themselves on the democratic axis of representative politics and those who more or less refuse to situate themselves there?*

FL: My problem as a non-philosopher is not to recreate the economy of intellectuals, to classify them, to sort them into two groups and to vary this distribution. Intellectuals see to that very well themselves in their current debates. I would simply like to relate them all – counselors to tyrants or to democracy, globalization activists, anti-globalization activists, alter-globalization activists, liberal or not – to a certain abstract and incomplete usage of the structure of philosophy (they only put some of its functions or effects into play and not others). This is why, as a non-philosopher, I would like to be careful about saying anything about these personalities. But look, of course as an ordinary citizen I have "my opinions," as we so provisionally say, a sad and fluctuating little thing which serves as grist for the mill precisely for the intellectuals threatened with unemployment. "A free man does not have opinions" (Valéry), certainly, but as the free man is today no longer much at work [*opératoire*], I would say "a non-philosopher only has opinions in order to transform them." The opinions of others and the non-philosopher's own are her material, at once her materials and her tools, but the treatment that she proposes is, of course, not an opinion. We can think highly of the intellectuals working with the rubbish of history, which they never stop recycling, but the Victim is not a piece of garbage and would have to determine the intellectual for another kind of treatment that engages the Victim directly as a subject.

PP: *Yes, but the philosopher can take responsibility for the Victim. He too has no opinions. He offers demonstrations, a conceptual logic . . .*

FL: If we just want to simply oppose demonstrations to opinions, then I fear that we are effectively still within the philosophical horizon. Demonstrations are perhaps necessary but they must apply to the opinions themselves, which are their object, and so depend on premises that aren't mathematical but rather are real. So, that said, I of course include philosophical theses, even the most abstract, within the sphere of opinions, those of the philosophers – this clears a supplementary step in the problematic of philosophy.

PP: *Can you state now what you mean by a philosophical genealogy? How is it established?*

FL: What we call philosophy is an extremely vague term, hazily maintained. Philosophy is first of all a verbal generality – one does philosophy. We don't really know what it means except that it designates academic study. We therefore have to look for some criterion, if there is one. And yet there is a criterion, but it's very complicated since it is precisely like a criterion for decriterialization; it auto-affects itself. Let's imagine an invariant, but one that is identical or co-extensive to its variations and which, furthermore, is not formal but claims to be of the Real, whatever the name of the Real. Of course the definitions of philosophy are programmed failures. If philosophy speaks of the intelligible, it itself is not intelligible, it functions above the intelligible . . .

PP: *Once we have located the structure of the basis of philosophy, what you call its invariants, we know who is a philosopher and who is not. But how do we recognize an intellectual?*

FL: The intellectual makes a certain usage of this structure. He begins with the selection of a function, the division of the basic dyad of philosophy's global structure. A large part of the intellectual posture results from this selection. Essentially isolating the duality's function, the separation of terms, he loses in the same moment the primordial sense of unity or the identity of the system. His work is, by definition, unfinished, interminable, much more than that of the philosopher. It is above all a thought of the understanding and close to the Enlightenment. Hence for the intellectual, the primacy of critique, the primacy of a certain conflictual nature, of clarification, of analysis, without utilizing these instruments in order to form any system. The philosopher and the intellectual begin with the same kind of work, but the philosopher completes this work in a system. They do not quite do the same job. Valéry said that the philosopher is someone who makes his empire after having made his revolution. The intellectual constantly makes his revolution but never constructs an empire. Or rather, if he tries to find a substitute for the empire of the system, then it is the mediatized system that he commits to. Will the intellectual be in reality the exact concept of the philosopher, his mediatized essence, the necessary synthesis for an excessive use of abstract understanding and of the system of representation that accompanies it, the penalty and fidelity of the contemporary philosopher? This misunderstanding maybe doesn't frighten the Eleatic Stranger but it does risk complicating our construction . . . We will have to take a closer look.

PP: *But the intellectual who has said his goodbyes as an intellectual (Régis Debray) and the one who has not (Bernard-Henri Lévy) both form and reset some of these relations. For one it is a way of carrying on, for the other it is a way of intervening, not just in general causes but in specific problems. We are not far from the specific intellectual of Michel Foucault. So there is a struggle between the general intellectual and the specific intellectual, more modest, more withdrawn, and who only intervenes on isolated problems.*

FL: In the past, the great intellectual figures knew how to synthesize justice and literature, sometimes politics, art . . . Now, effectively, the division is a little different, but not always. The general intellectuals inspire no confidence in me, their general competency is a waste and a poor use of philosophy and refers to no practice other than a media-friendly one. Undoubtedly media practices are becoming practices in themselves, with their artisans, experts, artists, and above all managers. However, there are some intellectuals who are coming back to more philosophico-scientific tasks, they have the urge to create a discipline, to take their place in the composition of the human sciences. It's necessary to considerably stretch the function of the intellectual, making that function global and making agents available who could very well come from collectives or associations, or even come from States. Being an intellectual is no longer a reserved function, it is also the condition through which the functions become more specific.

PP: *What do you think of Michel Foucault?*

FL: Foucault placed himself within the articulation of philosophy and history, a border which he always moved. He had been influenced by phenomenology, at a certain time, with a Heideggerian temptation, but in the end his philosophy is fundamentally Nietzschean. Already in Nietzsche's philosophy there was a certain kind of interest in archives, micro-history, genealogy, current events, and Foucault dug into this Nietzschean fissure. He radicalized Nietzsche's historicizing aspect by glossing over his most general philosophical presuppositions, magnified absolutely by Deleuze, without abandoning them. He theorized the intellectual, his practices, his actuality, but without reducing himself to that function. He's a Nietzschean journalist; he did, if we could put it this way, "High Journalism."

PP: *Foucault did speak about an ontology of the present and Giorgio Agamben evokes the political uses of Foucault.*

FL: Yes, I agree completely, but has philosophy ever made anything except ontologies of the present? Since Hegel, this is very clear-cut: philosophy is the analysis of the present and even of current events. We have to appeal to history for that, but history is reabsorbed in the present that it constitutes. An evaluation of philosophy is an impossible task because philosophy itself evaluates everything, so the philosophers content themselves with announcing various ends, of philosophy, of intellectuals, of art. Current events are carriers of death [*mortifère*] . . . in every sense of the term, various crimes, foreshadowed deaths, Ideas fall as fast as they rise. You understand that I have an urge to put the future in the helm, some would say, and to test a uchronic hypothesis against the embalmers and criminals who overcrowd the present scene. And, moreover, what if this flood of ideal cadavers carried along by the black river of History hid from us the river bottom, its bed lined with very human victims?

PP: *Jean-Claude Milner wrote a book in 2002 entitled* Existe-t-il une vie intellectuelle en France? *[Does an Intellectual Life Exist in France?]. The answer: no. He even advises young people to exile themselves from France. Additionally, he insists a great deal on this idea that Paris was an intellectual capital when it had something to say about the question of war and peace. There is, of course, the very symbolic example of Bergson who was an ambassador to President Wilson and who was the mediator for the intervention of the United States in 1917. There are also the examples of Simone Weil, Sartre, and Bertrand Russell who played a role beyond their own countries. Does this question of war, which has come back with the notion of a just war and the politics of American power, also fall under this philosophical genealogy?*

FL: Intellectuals and war ... I believe that it is also necessary to connect this question to the philosophical horizon. The problem is first one of philosophy, in the most noble sense, and war. I have always thought that philosophy was fundamentally polemical and agonistic (two distinct but convertible things) and that philosophy combined war and peace. Philosophy is always blended according to various proportions, it does not understand definitively unilateral determination but inscribes determination within a final horizon of convertibility. Even separated in the work of the intellectuals, warmongering and pacifism go hand in hand. War and peace are artifacts when separated, they are abstract effects of the philosophical order within which they are divided, but when isolated these are not fully philosophical positions.

PP: *Are there any thinkers or philosophers of war who displace the structure that you just mentioned?*

FL: Kant tried to break the cycle. Not only because he wrote "Perpetual Peace," but because he understood that perpetual war was the essence of ancient philosophy, what he called metaphysics, and that philosophy was being eaten up from the inside by a drive to auto-destruction. Philosophy is a palace in ruins, he said, and it is true that philosophy has been a site of demolition and also a site of reconstruction. Kant put some distance between himself and this conception of philosophy by trying to base it on science, in particular on Newton's mathematical physics. This is what allowed him to think or to believe that peace was possible, because with science we leave the closed sphere of philosophy, the sphere of the *polemos*. Everything that has come after Kant has only brought about a return to the spirit of war or in any case the blending of war and peace. Hegel and Nietzsche are almost greater philosophers than Kant in the sense that they realized the perfect system of philosophy. By returning to metaphysics in a certain way, not to its determined systems but to its spirit, they put war back in its inevitable place, within the Real and within thought, instead of in war. The system suspends war in the last moment, in the moments leading up to it, but ultimately it launches war again.

PP: *One could say that Bergson was a philosopher of peace, but one couldn't say that he was a thinker of peace. The question remains philosophical in Bergson. But Levinas, he was a thinker of peace.*

---

FL: The intellectual holds the middle between the religious or political thinker and the philosopher. We always attach a "regional" adjective to the thinker. The thinker is someone who works with the dynamic structure of philosophy but by finally twisting it much more than the intellectual. Rather, as it concerns him, the abstract intellectual works on an aspect that he takes to the absolute: division, critique. If he inevitably recovers the synthetic aspect, it's only under the unapparent form, that of the mediatized system. While the thinker is someone who introduces another point of view on philosophy. I think that these are closely linked to philosophy like Hamann, Jacobi, and Kierkegaard: in particular they introduced a religious point of view with regard to grand philosophical rationalism. Kant had Hamann, Fichte had Jacobi, Schelling and Hegel had Kierkegaard. So they are all dissenters – in this case, Lutherans. Hamann, for example, wrote a metacritique of the purism of pure reason.

PP: *What is it that differentiates philosophers and intellectuals in their relation to war?*

FL: A philosopher who rigorously thinks about his discipline, in referring to its ultimate foundations, knows that peace is armed, a suspension of war, and that there are unidentified wars. Agreements leave the balance of power suspended but also revive them. The intellectual enters into the conflict with the hope, however insane, of working to calm conflict down as if this were an absolute value. He gives himself the right to intervene in crises, wars, by postulating that his action will have the effect of clarification and so (believing as he does in an optimism in flowery words) the effect of regulation. There are two things that remain from the philosophical system in the work of the intellectuals: the initial choices of division and of critique. What remains of concrete philosophical practice is a mediation function, and a mediatized consummation of representation is the end or the telos for the intellectual, just as for the philosopher the end is the system. Peace for the intellectuals, like truth, like justice, remains ideal without any efficacy; they are references that are as much abstract as they are absolute. For the philosopher, the absolute is always relative. It always has a relationship to experience, it comes out of experience and becomes absolute. The intellectual doesn't have the patience of the concept.

PP: *And why do you say that non-philosophy is on the side of peace?*

FL: Because non-philosophy constitutes itself upon *radical identity which is distant or other* to the blend of war and peace specific to philosophy. What I call Man-in-person or Name-of-Man is necessarily peaceable rather than pacifist. He refuses to enter into the circuit of war and peace but he deals with it rather than it dealing with him. It is probably a utopia in action, performing itself as a utopia and uchronia. At bottom peace comes from the radical immanence which forms Man, and it comes to future blends of war and peace.

PP: *For a non-philosopher, is a just war possible?*

FL: The non-philosopher poses problems in terms of the usage of war-and-peace, but there is no absolute position of the one or the other as ideal. Peace is not an ideal in the sense that pacifism intends, because restoring peace absolutely is also a form of violence. "We will force them to make peace . . ." Of course, war is no longer an ideal, but there can be problems which may only be settled by war. The true problem of non-philosophy is one of usage, but determined as practice according to the Name-of-Man. There is a pragmatic of blending war and peace, which is his true pacifism.

PP: *In* Remnants of Auschwitz, *the Italian philosopher Giorgio Agamben writes: "The unprecedented discovery made by Primo Levi at Auschwitz concerns an area that is independent of every establishment of responsibility, an area in which Levi succeeded in isolating something like a new ethical element. Levi calls it the 'grey zone.' It is the zone in which the 'long chain of conjunction between Victim and executioner' comes loose, where the oppressed becomes oppressor and the executioner in turn appears as victim."[4] What do you think of this phrase? How do you approach the notion of responsibility? What meaning do you give it, precisely after Auschwitz?*

FL: To be honest, I am tired of "after Auschwitz," which has become a slogan. And "before Auschwitz," what happened, nothing, only accidents of history, just forerunners to the Shoah? Or was persecution at play?

---

[4] Giorgio Agamben, *Remnants of Auschwitz: The Witness and the Archive*, trans. Daniel Heller-Roazen (New York: Zone Books, 1999), p. 21.

---

The before interests me as much as the after. I think persecution is completely forgotten by the duty of memory, those persecutions of religious heretics, dualists, and gnostics. Victims are not "suitors," like there are suitors for the truth. This is the *substantia nigra* that flows through the veins of history. Still unimaginable crimes are for that matter readying themselves in its folds, still more invisible and more featureless, crimes according to the future. We will no longer know whether they are crimes against humanity, the human species, human life, crimes for which we will decidedly no longer have any criteria. So this is when being "an intellectual" will no longer be enough. As for the reversibility of persecutors and their victims, the logic of this circle has already been brought to light by Nietzsche and verifying it a bit more concretely is the only thing now called for; we will have to return to this.

PP: *In everything that you are saying, you put distance between it and every form of worldly engagement. We will have the opportunity to develop your conception of the victim, but would you say that there exists a non-philosophical conscience of the world like there exists a philosophical conscience?*

FL: Non-Philosophy is not a worldly engagement even if it constantly busies itself in the world and if it takes worldly engagement as its materials. Non-Philosophy is, in some way, a thought that has some affinity with the second degree of thought without being this second degree. Of course, conscience is engaged with immediate struggle, even with philosophical struggles, but the non-philosophical conscience – insofar as there is one – is not a reflection but a usage, a way of using, consummating and consuming the blend of contraries.

PP: *But, in war, do we die as a man or as a non-philosopher?*

FL: We die as a subject, not as Man-in-person (in my terms). But what is a Man? The non-philosopher, in the exact sense of the term, doesn't confuse himself with concrete men but he has the Name-of-Man in common with them. That's enough for any man to have the real possibility of being a non-philosopher even if he doesn't become one in his actions and in his thoughts on the battlefield.

PP: *Looking back, how have you experienced the American intervention in Iraq? Non-Philosopher that you are, what feelings are brought to the surface by this shock-and-awe war?*

FL: With bitterness of course, modesty also, and a growing distrust of the intellectuals who are once again taking their places. It was kind of a crucial experiment, as they say in physics. We have been manipulated by the diabolical trio, our three Fates: arrogance, lying, triumphant force. These Medusa figures which seemed for a moment to be absent from our everyday lives have returned "in the real," as Lacan would say. Now, more than ever, the only practice still possible – no joke – is a utopia in action, as a practice of thought.

PP: *We can now move to serious matters. You have made your intentions clear and I get the feeling that I have tortured you by asking you about current events. It remains for us to implement your way of thinking, to get down to what you mean by the dominant intellectual, the determined intellectual, and to clarify what you call a new experience of utopia.*

# The Name-of-Man or
# the Identity of the Real

PP: *After this introduction to the material and before starting with your description of the dominant intellectual, it seems necessary to me to mark off the boundaries of your field of reflection and sketch a few lines of introduction to non-philosophy. The term is intriguing, it cannot be understood without some explication of what you call the Real, this heretical and separated Real that you present in* Future Christ *as "a definitively lost model of thought [. . .] a Western outside-memory, a loss without possible return, an im-memorial paradigm."[1] Later on I will ask you more prosaic questions and I will act as the advocate for philosophy and ordinary politics, but first you have to specify the nature of your heresy. Your experience of the Real includes overcoming the simple philosophical desire for the Real. This requires some clarification.*

---

[1] François Laruelle, *Future Christ: A Lesson in Heresy*, trans. Anthony Paul Smith (London and New York: Continuum, 2010), pp. 42–3.

---

FL: As a non-philosopher, I accept that there is some irreducible and definitive presupposed in thought, and this is necessary in order to defeat idealism and to think according to the Real – for example, thinking according to the Victim (if what is presupposed is the Victim) rather than according to philosophy. The experience of the Real by which we will be able to overcome the simple philosophical desire for the Real is that of a presupposed, and that changes everything. Not an always more originary experience, but one presupposed. How will you think if you have something presupposed? Here this is called, or is symbolized, as *Name-of-Man* or, by way of its content, as Man-in-person. We will come back to this. Radical human identity is separated from the World [*monde*], un-clean [*im-monde*] as Lacan would say, or holy. But holiness is decidedly subject to too much misunderstanding.

PP: *There is not one conception, but several, of the Real in philosophy. This isn't without serious problems!*

FL: There are three major conceptions of the Real that are philosophical. For the first philosophers, the model is consciousness of itself or the distance of being from itself. This is a Real grounded upon the unfurling of some distance from oneself. The Real is what is given to itself but by crossing a distance. Perception is the basic empirical model for the philosophers who are irredeemably visual instead of spiritual. Hence, the Real is the philosophical desire for the real.

PP: *And the Real in psychoanalysis?*

FL: The second conception that we have to deal with is that of the unconscious. The clearest conception of this point of view is of course that of Lacan. The Real is then at the limit of the unconscious (of the symbolic) and provides its unmovable weight. Lacan distinguished the symbolic and the Real, and of course the imaginary. The symbolic is of the order of knowing but the real is at the limit of the symbolic. It has an aspect through which it exceeds the symbolic. There is then in Lacan a fundamental ambiguity between knowing and the Real. This is not at all the philosophical situation, which is idealist, so the unconscious Real is no longer just of the order of consciousness. If consciousness is its own ecstatic movement towards itself, the unconscious Real is always "in its place," Lacan says. He ended up filling out the unconscious, even if he hesitated a great deal between several conceptions of the Real; he gave it its true dimension which is not the symbolic. It is the Real which gives the unconscious a weight which is irreducible to knowledge, which means primarily to philosophical consciousness.

PP: *But is the Real, for Lacan, given under the form of a drive?*

FL: Yes and no, but either way it is always a movement of transcendence (albeit a move "to the same place"). This presupposed is unstable and has the tendency to slip about on every instance of the unconscious, that's all that interests me. You understand why I am looking for a stable or immanent presupposed. Just as the victims are reabsorbed and dissolved in history, or even, to a greater extent, humans are the same within the sciences and anthropology. One and the other, the same, can only be saved if we posit the symbol of their irreducibility with a decision that is exasperating for the revisionism of history and the sciences. Non-Philosophy's unique objective is to struggle against the revisionism of philosophy and the sciences through a nonrevisionist practice of their discourse, the only one that we have at our disposal ... What kind of usage of philosophical or analytic language must work or be reworked according to this presupposed of the Real? There is a Real which is one presupposed, so what does it result in for thought?

PP: *A third conception is then possible. The non-philosophical concept of the Real is neither that of philosophy nor that of psychoanalysis. Is this the idea of a radical immanence* and not an absolute immanence?

FL: In effect, consciousness is absolute: it posits itself, makes itself objective and masters itself. On the other hand, the radical Real does not even return to the same place, it is only able to be grasped in-Real and we cannot understand it through a concept since it is only imma-nent, it is only possible to give its symbol, and draw the consequences that it implies. It is a presupposed, we can only bring it out within declarations [*énoncés*] that are new ways of using these philosophical declarations. But we will not say that this is only an empty or formal symbol, the Real is an "instance," even if it is the "last." The Name-of-Man designates that there is something simply human and not anthropological in man and it designates this as Man-in-person.

---

PP: *It is important, I believe, to immerse oneself in this vision of the Real as presupposed. It determines your approach to the question of the intellectuals. The Real, in your work, is like a given-without-givenness. We are then outside the field of phenomenology. You have to confess this isn't easy to grasp.*

FL: The Real is a being-given without there having been an operation of givenness. Of course, that is a very paradoxical abstraction, it requires an effort of thought. We cannot grasp it without escaping from the classical representation of identity, or the contemporary representation of alterity. I take literally Nietzsche's idea that philosophy is a way of denigrating the Real and vengeance against it. I have tried to develop language which registers the fact that the Real is unrepresentable. More exactly still, I would not say that it is representable or unrepresentable, but instead that the Real is that which = X, determining in-the-last-instance a subject *for* the relation of representation and the unrepresentable proper to philosophy, a subject for the relation of two signifiers. One can see the distance between this and Lacan's "the signifier represents a subject for another signifier." Certainly, but it is the Real that determines this signifying relationship as a subject. What is representable or unrepresentable is no longer the problem. No longer do I define it according to one of the parts of the contradiction.

PP: *This given-without-givenness has nothing to do with the field of experience and thus to related philosophical representations . . . So why have you just spoken to me about vengeance?*

FL: Vengeance is a structural trait of philosophy and the dominant intellectual. This doesn't psychologize it, vengeance is a concept that can itself take on a philosophical status. There are very few philosophers who really speak about vengeance and who try to clarify it – Nietzsche and Heidegger. So, it's a relatively contemporary way of thinking. Philosophy is vengeance against the Real because it is vengeance against itself, against what it believes to be the Real and then precisely because it believes itself to be this Real that it wants to repress, so that the Real is not repressible or forgettable, just foreclosed. Philosophy is inseparable from this relationship of self-destruction that moves right into nihilism. This is what follows from a movement which begins at least with Plato's *Parmenides* but has above all taken its full form with the transcendental dialectic of Kant, with the idea that philosophy is appearance and transcendental illusion. All of this has been reworked by Hegel and Nietzsche until they arrived at the crucial problem of nihilism. In short, vengeance is a concept best served cold, it is a vengeful concept . . .

Additionally, vengeance implies that justice and nonjustice function circularly. Justice presents itself as interrupting the circle of vengeance, an eye for an eye, the circle that goes from the individual victim to the individual criminal. But in reality justice is only a mediation and plateau, a halt to vengeance. The problem of justice, as Nietzsche called it, is one of finding some equivalence between the crime and the reparation or punishment of the criminal, all the while deriving from the Victim the power to punish. But this support for some mediation or even for some "differe/ance" in the circle of vengeance does not destroy the circle itself.

---

It only opens it up a little more. In a continuous way, philosophy reconstitutes the circle of autocritique, the reciprocity of contraries. This is not an eye for an eye, but it is the superior form of this law within thought. Philosophy is what it makes of itself, it heals itself by way of the wound it inflicts on itself. I only see an extension of the circle of vengeance in this reciprocity that can stretch so far as to be a reversibility. The intellectual manipulates this circle and gets his revenge on reality through the critique but, in fact, he himself reproduces this war at a higher level. The problem will be finding a status for the Victim that does not insert her into the circle once again, something you also spoke about when you quoted Primo Levi, the circle or the fold of persecution which binds the persecutor and his victim.

PP: *You're moving a bit too quickly for me. A number of jurists and philosophers are today wondering about criminal reason. The "truth and reconciliation" commission, set up in 1995 in South Africa, has attempted precisely to break the diabolical circle of tormenter and victim by refusing the break between morality and legality and by attempting to institute on a case-by-case basis the reporting of crimes committed by the Afrikaners. It's a first in the history of humanity!*

FL: I don't deny those efforts, that would be ridiculous. It's necessary to break down in each of them what is still philosophizable or apparent, and what begins to break or displace this circle. Understand that I am making a critique of philosophical appearance, it is an appearance but an objective one.

---

PP: *Will courage, in your work, be associated with vengeance?*

FL: There is violence and also vengeance in the philosophical ethics of heroism. I would link this to the theme of auto-defense that I have critiqued in *Future Christ*. Philosophy is in a state of auto-defense. It wants to put in place a logic of action and reaction, a logic of reflection, so an eye for an eye at a higher level. Non-Philosophy renounces auto-defense, not in favor of a heterodefense by intermediary advocates, but for a defense of thought that only authorizes itself right at the Real [*au Réel près*]. Defending itself under the presupposed of the Real, this is not auto-defense or vengeance, it is *a priori* defense – for that matter a fundamental concept for the defense of victims. To right the wrong committed against the Victim, but the presupposed of the inescapable existence of the Victim this time as Name-of-Man. The reparation cannot be the Name-of-Man's effacement within memory and its "duty" as is the case, more or less, in our philosophical or religious vision of the World.

PP: *Is this then a new universal, defending thought right at the Real. A unilateral universal that, despite everything, claims to join men together. So then what is it that distinguishes the non-philosophical universal from the universal of the intellectuals?*

FL: The defense of thought against philosophical appearance is what constitutes this difference, but as determined by the Real. Thought, which is the subject, what I call the Stranger-subject, defends herself against the World and against history as philosophizables while also making a use out of them, but it is the Real that is determinant for this struggle. On the other hand, the universal of dominant intellectuals is itself dominant, its auto-defense is like the wrong side of the spirit of conquest. The dominant universal is the community of philosophers which has its roots in the Greek *polis*, and which in Kant gives us "thinking in common" and the modern intellectual of the Enlightenment, as well as public space. The community is then the Real which precedes the Name-of-Man and reduces it to anthropology and humanism. But what I call the Real is not universal in the sense of a global nature and totality, nor for that matter as partial and "molecular" (Deleuze). It is uni-versal, meaning unilateral. The Real does not fall under the encompassing universal of the dominant intellectuals. I used to say that this was the radical individual [*individu*], but I wouldn't say it any more, the term "individual" [*individu*] being overly charged already. Of course, all of the difficulty here is that the Real is *in* [*en*], and not the Real *for* [*à*], which makes it unthinkable and unrepresentable. If there is a reconstitution of some universal that brings it closer to the classical type, then it is the Stranger-subjects within their multiplicity, Strangers in the sense of being unilateral in relation to the World. There are several conceptions of the universal and most of the time, in philosophy, when we think a universal, we think totality, a global nature, a world, *polis*, *physis*, categories ... even though I take it in the literal sense of the term, *uni-versal*.

PP: *What do you mean when you say that the non-philosophical Real is not an abstraction but one abstract?*

FL: The Real is abstract but without an operation of abstraction. We cannot say that Man-in-person *exists*. He is real but he does not exist. The Real is on this side of essence and existence, of being and nothingness. It is what = X, determining a subject from the balance of being and nothingness which is proper to philosophy. So I always return to the problem of the practice of thought. I refuse to define those first terms I give myself or I define them only in an axiomatic way, meaning implicitly. So I can say that Man is that X which determines-in-the-last-humaneity (and not "humanity") the subject, and does so on the basis of conflicts or philosophical contradictions; or even that the Victim-in-person is who determines in-the-last-humaneity the relation of the intellectual to victims given as an element of history. I prefer "humaneity" to designate the human Real rather than the abstraction "humanity."

PP: *Can you unpack this formula: man is real but he does not exist?*

FL: I distinguish the Real from existence, from essence or from Being. If we assume that the Real exists, then it is no longer the real, it is reality. Historical, empirical, mundane reality, within space and within time, exists or is denied, reduced to nothingness and no longer exists. It is very difficult to find a category with which to define the Real, because all the philosophical categories apply for Being, or the One insofar as categories about it exist, or apply for Nothingness. The Real no longer puts up with these categories, it cannot be said in the terms of World, History, or Truth. In order to exist, it must step out of itself. But by definition the Real is unable to step outside of itself, unlike Being which leaves itself if only to show itself to itself. But the Real does not reveal itself to itself from the exterior of itself, and the intellectuals will find themselves definitively amidst finitude, without any possible glimpse [*survol*] of the victims. It is a point of immanence, and yet . . . This is a bad definition because a point of immanence is something one can project into space and turn into a transcendent thing, something like the Neoplatonic One. We could say that it is a consistent interiority, but interiority is also a term to rework because one kind of interiority is imagined under a psychological form. You can see that as soon as I give a definition it is a failure. We have to refuse the temptation or appearance of definition. Man-in-Man is not a psychological subject or a political subject. This is the presupposed, the condition, which negatively determines or determines in-the-last-instance a subject for all the games of giving definitions and predicates that drives [*font mouvoir*] philosophy. I can't say it or unsay it any other way.

PP: *So, once the philosophical unthoughts are done away with, what method do you use in order to describe this non-philosophical "victim?" What do you do so as not to lapse into a language game? Once belief and the refusal of belief are swept away, what can be glimpsed of the Victim-in-person? She is not uniquely an effect of language and neither is this a modification of philosophical relation.*

FL: One could say that it is an effect of language, that it is not language which itself produces this effect, because it will still be philosophy. This effect is determined by

Man-in-person *qua* Real. This effect can on the whole be designated by the symbol of the Name-of-Man. It is an axiomatic effect, not logico-formal but transcendental because it deals with reality in general, it is determined by the Real and is directed towards the reality of victims ... It is a transformation, not a modification of philosophical, worldly, or historical relations.

PP: *But then, in the same way that some have ironically talked about the proofs for the existence of God, are there then no proofs for the existence of man?*

FL: Fortunately not! The Name-of-Man, this is neither God nor the name of God. You want a proof so that you can know that you exist or that you are within Being or within the World, but not in order to know that you are the last presupposed possible for every thought and that you are only such without yourself being this thought. There are no exterior proofs or criteria for Man-in-person, this is what is signified by the Name-of-Man. If one such proof existed, it would be the death of Man, the ultimate persecution, the last hostage taken by philosophy and the sciences, the triumph of humanism, that old embalmer. The subject may be a hostage, meaning Man when he begins to exist as a relation in the World, for example in a relation to concrete victims. We are going to have to work from the discourse of an asceticism and a quasi-psychoanalysis when we want to speak of the Real, because the Real disputes all forms of the concept or definition and reduces them to the state of an objective appearance. The Real is not a problem and in one sense it doesn't interest me. What does interest me is how to deal with victims, how to release them from philosophy, from science, or from their aestheticization, but under that necessary condition – which is not a sufficient one – that the presupposed Real is. Incidentally, this is precisely not a philosophical presupposition.

PP: *Yes, but you said as well that it isn't an unknown but an irreducible kind of knowing. If it isn't a problem or a question, then we cannot relate it to anxiety or to a will to know. So what can we relate it to?*

FL: The Real is neither a knowing consciously nor a knowing unconsciously, because the unconscious is also a form of knowing – a logic, for example. It is what determines a subject in-the-last-humaneity for the relation between consciousness and the unconscious. So if I nevertheless wanted to indicate this Real within the order of knowing, as knowledge of the third kind, and it must be such, then I will say that the Real is an *unlearned knowledge*, rather than a "learned ignorance." Unlearned means that it is neither an expert knowledge nor a taught knowledge. It is non-taught knowledge, it gives its unilateral identity to a subject.

PP: *This is very privative, it cuts off the philosophical impulse.*

FL: But how would you like to define a knowledge that is primitive and void of determinations, even more than the first, since it possesses primacy only over the subject? This is the form or concrete substance of other forms of knowing, recognized as the substance of the World.

PP: *This cuts off the philosophical impulse and any impulse altogether! Such unlearned knowing does not by definition set me down the path of my desire. Even the notion of desire becomes suspect. From the perspective of unlearned knowing, what would you put in place of desire?*

FL: The Real doesn't cut off this impulse, this isn't a supplementary cut into philosophical desire. On the contrary, it manifests desire in cutting it, undoubtedly, but in cutting it, if I can put it this way, from an identity or in setting it "in" identity. It manifests desire but deprived of its pretension to be All-desire. I will not follow this ideology of All-desire that there is in a certain psychoanalysis but that cannot be found in Lacan – or can be, but in a much more nuanced way.

PP: *What are the points of difference between yourself and psychoanalysis? You say that it is going to be necessary to carry out a psychoanalysis of the intellectuals, can you clarify what you mean by that?*

FL: The determined intellectual constantly passes through a quasi-psychoanalysis of the dominant intellectual. The relationship is quite difficult to establish because the project (this being one formulation among others) is one of an elaboration of concepts with an analytic allure but adapted to intellectual activities, not simplistic concepts or on philosophy's level. I can only utilize the language of psychoanalysis, but in transforming it and molding it into what I call non-analysis. A psychoanalysis that is non-Lacanian and non-Freudian must utilize the language of Lacan and Freud, their concepts, their problems, but these are transformed under a presupposed and a causality different from those of the unconscious. If I transform this language, as I attempted to do in *Théorie des Étrangers*,[2] under the term of "non-psychoanalysis," I am going to get concepts such as the enjoyed-without-*jouissance* [*jouissans-jouissance*], etc. These concepts, some of them fabricated whole-cloth and others transformed from Lacan's work, will provide the structure of a psychoanalysis which would be truly adequate to philosophical objectives and capable of bringing ruin to these objectives as much as universalizing them. Without all that, this project would be a deconstruction – the Real is not the same one that we find in deconstruction, one which is very close to the letter of the Real in psychoanalysis. If twentieth-century Continental philosophy could be summed up as a conflict between philosophy and psychoanalysis, then my problem has been to avoid this conflict and elaborate a science of men [*science des hommes*] which would be capable of confronting philosophy in its pretension to the Real and in the *jouissance* of the Real. The simple relation of psychoanalysis and philosophy is bound to be war. It is impossible for them to agree except by mutually distorting themselves. If enemies mutually distort themselves, then their conflict no longer presents anything of interest. The real struggle assumes the full recognition of the enemy and in this case the full recognition of philosophy. What we can't do is reduce it to a system of drives [*pulsions*] because if it were only that, like what we see in Nietzsche, it would

---

[2] François Laruelle, *Théorie des Étrangers: Science des hommes, démocratie, non-pyschanalyse* (Paris: Kimé, 1995).

only be called a psychological critique. Philosophy is not a psychological or instinctual [*pulsionnel*] event, at least not in its being, it is transcendental, autonomous, it is an ideal system and it has to find the means of confronting itself with that consistency. Non-Philosophy is a way of taking up the problems of the world, of history, of philosophy, rather than those of simple consciousness, as psychoanalysis does, but it is a way of taking them up which has some relationship with psychoanalysis. It is not about transposing psychoanalysis, as if it exists like a certain science of the mind, onto intellectual work. That can be done, but it is not very interesting. Intellectuals have a unique way of thinking; we have to invent the "psychoanalysis" adequate to that way of thinking.

PP: *I notice that you have gotten rid of "the session." Is your psychoanalysis also of the third kind?*

FL: It is still a practice, even of the third kind, an analysis of philosophical kinds of resistance. But it is not psychological, and the practice is broader than the "session" with its temporal scansion.

PP: *So is the unrepresentable Real equally irreducible? Can we say that, for philosophy, nothing is irreducible, so that, for you, there exists an irreducible human? This is maybe the time for us to speak a little more about this irreducibility, about this Man-in-person that constitutes the core of your approach to thinking.*

FL: Of course, the premise of the general reducibility of sense content and the reality of the world to philosophy, and principally of man, the *philosophizability* of the Name-of-Man, is what I am fighting against. This is what I call the Principle of Sufficient Philosophy, which means that philosophy postulates that it can give meaning, reality, and truth, *de facto* or *de jure*, to everything that appears, and even give meaning, reality, and truth to the Real. Philosophy postulates a universal philosophizability. The funny thing about this situation is that philosophy always finds itself at one and the same time too late – to philosophize the things that are already produced – and too early, but it never truly coincides with the birth of things, it is never there. Non-Philosophy produces a concept of the "radical beginning" but suspends it in Man-in-person as definitively Other or separated, or even "future." This future is not anticipated, it is the way of acting or determining from the Real.

PP: *The Real or reality? These are not the same thing for you then? You say that the Real doesn't interest you. That's not quite right: "human identity" is what you have fastened your concern to.*

FL: Human identity is no longer the coincidence of opposites, which is formed against a background of transcendence. Some philosophers have approached this radical immanence: Michel Henry for example, if not Husserl. But here it is truly an immanence which defies representation, in that it affects from an *a priori* future that is void of determinations, void of form, even the form of ekstasis [*extase*] and of representation. It is precisely because it cannot represent itself that it comes to modify representation. In a way, we would better understand what non-philosophy is if we have always under our gaze the model of psychoanalysis with, on the one hand, the ruses of consciousness, the complexity of its evasions, its most twisted thoughts, and, on the other hand, the work of analysis. Man-in-Man is the Real which, instead of being still transcendent to knowledge like Lacan's real, is radically immanent "to itself." But hold on! "To itself" is a dangerous formulation, because there is no "itself" preformed in which immanence would find accommodation, which would mean that there would be a double immanence. It's the inherence of man, not to himself but to Man, that is sufficient to define immanence.

PP: *Essentially, what do you keep of Marx and Freud?*

FL: From Freud – well, more precisely, like many of my contemporaries, from Lacan's reading of Freud – I essentially retain the attempt to subvert philosophical authority by way of a discipline – I am saying a discipline and not a science – which at once integrates philosophical elements and scientific elements. In any case, this is very clear in Marx as well. It is a discipline that has, in a certain way, two faces. Historical materialism (if it is still permissible to talk about historical materialism without inviting sarcasm) is supposed to be a discipline which is neither a philosophy nor a science but a philosophy and science at the same time. Maybe it has failed as science and as philosophy – that is quite possible – but then, the whole problem is one of radicalizing the general conditions under which such a thought or such a discipline is possible. I find this radicalization partly in Lacan. Non-Philosophy has rediscovered, in its own way, that reflection upon the philosophical act and some of its themes – for example, Marx's theories of productive forces or the infrastructure/base, Lacan's theory of the real. Of course, the concept of the Real for non-philosophy is not exactly that of productive forces or that of the Lacanian real, but it is a general theoretical apparatus which has a "family resemblance" with theirs.

PP: *In fact, don't you separate yourself more from Lacan on the question of language than on the question of the Real?*

FL: On the question of the relation between the Real and language. Actually, I don't assign the same status that Lacan does either to the Real or to language. The Real is in-Real, without which it would be defined by its "being-in-the-same-place," and the hold of the Real over the symbolic happens through what I call cloning. Cloning replaces the knot or the major Lacanian apparatus in three-to-four branches (or boughs) which must be tied into topological transcendence. I do not tie things together, I clone them, and I contrast cloning to tying knots. Tying things together is necessary when there is some exteriority of authoritative bodies [*instances*] or some determinate transcendence, but for non-philosophy there is no longer this exteriority of authoritative bodies, which is the surest sign of philosophy.

PP: *But is there a point of origin in the inscribing of your Real's irreducibility in the history of the human subject? It is an experience that anyone could have: when babies come into the world, they are never already fully within the world. Is it that this baby, this child, before language, has the experience of this irreducibility? Is this a point of origin in relation to the birth of the human subject or is it a stage linked to the human species?*

FL: An immensely extensive and deep question. Let's start with the Name-of-Man and the Stranger-subject. I don't say that the subject encounters language, this is not a problem for me because I do not think in terms of the subject, which is only an effect. I think and speak first in terms of "man" and then of the subject, whereas Lacan advances, like a lot of contemporary philosophers, the notion of the subject, which in a certain way will exhaust man in his relation to the symbolic and then to the Real. The imaginary, through the subject, finally completes what Lacan may still understand by "man." The reason for this is a hasty or ill-founded critique of humanism. I try to provide a specific status, original to man as Man-in-person, and so consequently the subject has a derivative function, that of the relations of speech [*parole*] and action, functional and determined relations to the World in-the-last-humaneity.

There is no question that at a certain point we are born or become men as a subject. Not because we will forever be a man, that doesn't mean anything, but because we all have the negative possibility of determining our subject's relations to language and to history in a human way. That does not mean that we necessarily actualize it, but we can do it. Altogether this results in the following theory of birth. It is not necessary to pose the problem of the birth of Man within history or within time, this philosophico-common problem is absurd and unleashes a torrent of aporias and contradictions.

Regarding the birth of the subject, we can posit it but only with a great deal of nuance. The subject determined by Man is not the play between an operation of birth and a subject which is subjected to the passion of being born. It isn't a duality of that kind. The subject which is born is literally and above all else the New-Born, he who is born without birth. The subject is produced within birth, within the biological order, as a man in a World system. As Stranger-subject, he is born-without-birth from Man. This is what forms the miraculously human character of the child. And this is birth through cloning. In short – for a word to the wise is enough – cloning means nothing for Man, but it does mean something for the subject . . .

PP: *If I have understood correctly, you take a step beyond (or stop short of) the orphan unconscious (Deleuze). But what is your negation based on? Is it not grounded by Nothingness (Sartre), is it not actualized by what Alain Badiou calls the "reverse" [envers] of the World? Where is it found?*

FL: Precisely not the "reverse" [*envers*] but the "inverse" [*invers*]. The Real is an inversion of philosophy, but a radical inversion. The reverse is still a phenomenon of appearance within the World, as Badiou says. The "inverse" is an identity separated from the World, it is the effect of the Real upon the World.

PP: *Every subject is a New-Born – does that mean that every subject can be born anew as when Kafka said that he was not yet born?*

---

FL: Saying that one is not yet born involves the idea of a becoming, of birth as becoming. The Greeks by contrast said that they are actually born too much. For some, the great calamity for man is being born; for others, it is not yet being born. But the problem is not birth's anticipation or delay, for this is always a philosophical problem and one that gives way to some antithetical. We have the possibility of carrying out our humaneity as a new-born subject, this is the condition of our dis-alienation.

PP: *What do you mean by cloning?*

FL: If the Real is one presupposed, I must formulate my statements according to that presupposed. What I call cloning is the mechanism of the presupposed and its effect. Philosophy does not ask itself what the means of acting from the irreducible presupposed are, philosophy raises this up into a presupposition. So non-philosophy is the radical identity or the identity in-the-last-instance of a slow passage, always starting again from philosophy. This passage is blocked, so to speak, or carries the concrete mark of the Name-of-Man. Philosophers would say that non-philosophy conjugates a duality of radicality and a programmatic passage. It's not quite like that. This duality is unilateral, meaning that the passage is immediately transformed and understood under the Real's presupposed. It is important to understand that non-philosophy is that-which-I-do-in-saying and not just what I say, which could always be taken hold of again by philosophy. It is what I do with the language of philosophy and "from" this language. We don't have to project an image of non-philosophy

into some new heaven – a Platonic one, for example.
Non-Philosophy is a practice and an immanent practice. This is what screens out a lot of philosophers,
because philosophers always project something or
desire it. I don't have the desire for the Real, I say that
Man is the Real, that we are the Real. It doesn't impress
itself upon its object like the mark of an artisan, or like
the signifier, it gives or manifests this "object" with
the form of immanence or from the identity that it is.
Philosophical deception really reveals itself in Hegel
who says "we philosophers," when he should have said
"we humans."

PP: *Do you insist on speaking about this as cloning?*

FL: It's not the biotechnological version of cloning, that's
for sure! Though we should be under no illusions about
the possibility of stopping this version of cloning. I don't
understand how people can get so morally bothered by
cloning since we know that everything that is technically
possible eventually ends up happening. Cloning will
happen – it happens under forms that are imaginary,
mediatized, and delirious-sectarian, but it will also end
up happening in forms that are more moderate, more
therapeutic. The prudence of non-philosophy follows
from the logic of the "worst necessary" – this is not
the principle of the "best possible" but the principle of
the worst ("you ain't seen nothing yet"): it is a great
metaphysical principle which can simulate the process
of the *cogito* and at the same time destroy it. That said,
what I call cloning is not biological – which is to say
inhuman – but is more the essence of human action.
It's not the manufacture of a double for some existing

reality, under an identity which would be common to them. It is identity itself, meaning the Real, that is this immanent double forged with the material furnished by philosophy. The clone that I speak about is not an extra-terrestrial, it is extraworldly. Even "extraworldly" is not the best formula because it lets one assume that first there is the World and then comes Man. From the outset Man puts the World to the test before the World tests Man – the World as already given in the human mode. This is what causes the human subject, Man as Stranger-subject, to be thrown necessarily into the World, more so than Heidegger ever imagined. The Name-of-Man symbolizes this righteousness which will go from utopia to the World.

PP: *Can you say something else about the extraworldly?*

FL: It is the term "extra" which doesn't work. It still indicates a kind of transcendence in which thought posits the World and then man beyond the World. It is still what philosophers do. I do not want to make that gesture, because Man is the element through which I think as a subject. This is it, radical inherence, so it is impossible to survey [*survoler*] the World; we only approach the World from the identity of a future-in-person who is never a projection [*un surplomb*] from it.

PP: *What do you mean when you say that it is the Real which produces this double?*

FL: Non-Philosophy is the clone of philosophy, the New-Born. Non-Philosophy is produced by the effect of the presupposed Real within philosophy. The approach is relatively complicated, but we could summarize it in this way. Non-Philosophical statements are clones of philosophical or analytic statements – clones which are not doubles or exact reproductions of philosophy. Certainly not. It is only the identity of the Real which allows us to break with the idea of the mirror, of reflection, of the exact double. Non-Philosophy is not identical to philosophy, it is produced by the introduction of Identity itself into philosophical material, and the philosophical material does not know about this Identity, contrary to what common sense believes. Philosophy desires identity but does not know it. If we introduce identity in flesh and blood, in actuality, into philosophy, then the clone is produced. Would that be the attack of the clones?

PP: *Identity – this is the identity of the Real?*

FL: Yes, of course. There is no identity, in the strong sense of the term, which would not be simple desire or image, except for the Real. It is the Real that is able to be defined by its identity. I do not define it by its alterity as the psychoanalyst does, even though the latter says that the Real returns to the same place. But Lacan just did not get to the bottom of immanence, he was happy with the Real in its own place, within spatiality or on the "other scene." Since the concern here is with the intellectuals, it is important to be precise that this radical identity – without the slightest fissure or even spatiality – is the surest destruction of demands for recognition of "identity" . . .[3]

PP: *That's good news.*

---

[3] Laruelle is making a reference to the groups of the extreme Right, a reference that would be clear to his French readers. These groups, represented in France by intellectuals like Alain de Benoist who helped to found the New Right movement, argue for a strongly nationalistic sense of identity which sees forms of non-European and sometimes European immigration as a threat. Here identity is taken as transcendent, essentialist, and nationalistic and not at all immanent. [Translator's note.]

# Portrait of the
# Dominant Intellectual

PP: *We can start on the portrait of the dominant intellectual. In fact, he has all the traits of the intellectual just as sociology or journalism defines him: a true Proteus who changes himself according to the situation. Engaged, radical, specific, he always holds his course towards justice. How do you define what characterizes him?*

FL: The portrait of the dominant intellectual, which I will later contrast with the determined intellectual, can be characterized along several points. First, he has some philosophical basis, a cause which is specific to him or, better still, a principal affect. This principal affect is the primacy of division, the primacy of the rupture which is over unity and over the system. So much so that philosophy, in the full concept of its practice, is pushed into the background, in danger of becoming repressed. But as it is a forced hand, it returns under two concealed forms that constitute symptoms – we have seen them, mediation and the mediatized. The second point is that the primacy of division, which signals the intellectual's abstract character, must necessarily be clothed with a more empirical, more historical existence, so much so that this abstraction always has some ideological aspect for politics, morality, art, law. This complementary empirical aspect provides for the exercise of analysis or the division of its material means of existence. The third point is that of justice, which is certainly the dominant value for the "humanitarian" intellectual, a value favored at the expense of the ultimate end of philosophy: man. This way of conceiving justice makes it dominant in relation to man itself – this is one of the problems linked to the intellectual's abstraction. Fourth, the intellectual has causes other than justice to support: the earth, the land, blood, race, freedom of thought, the proletariat, human rights, etc., these are the values which motivate, foremost, his action and give him the opportunity to practice. So that the intellectual depends always on values and causes that he defends as absolutes and that he refuses to question. This is also true for academic intellectuals, Raymond Aron for example, who rests upon sociology and defends a kind of critical thinking and understanding that is close to the Enlightenment.

PP: *The 1972 conversation between Michel Foucault and Gilles Deleuze is entitled "Intellectuals and Power." It is situated in a moment in which the function of the intellectual is in the process of changing. Foucault sets out the great moments of the past: the Commune, 1940, etc. Here is what he wrote: "The intellectual was rejected and persecuted at the precise moment when the facts became incontrovertible, when it was forbidden to say that the emperor had no clothes. The intellectual spoke the truth to those who had yet to see it, in the name of*

*those who were forbidden to speak the truth: he was
conscience, consciousness, and eloquence. In the most
recent upheaval [1968] the intellectual discovered that
the masses no longer need him to gain knowledge. They
know perfectly well, without illusion; they know far
better than he and they are certainly capable of expressing themselves."*[1] *This was a moment in which we could
no longer speak. Foucault opposes, on the one hand,
the intellectual engaged in the name of some raising of
the peoples' consciousness and, on the other hand, the
specific intellectual who demands a new organization
of theory and practice. The expression "the indignity of
speaking for others" returns in several refrains. So this
is, in 1972, a moment in the changing role of the intellectual. Do you feel inspired by it?*

FL: It was the time when I myself spoke of the masses
and the people as a multitude. In a more contemporary
vocabulary – and at the same time paradoxically more
Platonic – we could say that the people can be inspiring.
This entire thematic, even that of popular inspiration,
remains present and necessary for me but I would like
to move it onto another theoretical terrain. Taken in the
way that you evoked it, I think it is quite situational and
rather naive, leftist but not without equivocation, in its
refusal of mediation. On this point may I recall an old
book, *Nietzsche contra Heidegger,*[2] in which I tried to

---

[1] "Intellectuals and Power: A Conversation between Michel Foucault and
Gilles Deleuze" in Michel Foucault, *Language, Counter-Memory, Practice:
Selected Essays and Interviews,* edited by Donald F. Bouchard (Ithaca, NY:
Cornell University Press, 1980), p. 207. [Translation slightly modified.]
[2] François Laruelle, *Nietzsche contra Heidegger: Thèses pour une politique
nietschéenne* (Paris: Payot, 1977).

get the most out of the proximity within which Nietzsche tangled revolution and fascism together? But my problem is no longer that one at all. Whether you defend a certain popular spontaneity taken up by the intellectuals or you give them a role as scouts, this changes the way in which they position themselves within history, but this does not change their status much. In these two extreme cases, they remain in the service of a philosophy which determines them – admittedly, more or less "close" to the people. What real service can they be put to – it will no longer be in the service of philosophy, its humanism or substitutes, the people, the plebs, minorities, masses – what cause is able to determine their concrete practice? I am not looking to position the intellectual along a philosophical spectrum, no longer concerned with knowing whether he is an intellectual who is for the most part Nietzschean or whether he is instead someone with Marxist tendencies. My problem has been placing him back within the context of fundamental philosophical presuppositions [*presupposés*], but in order to find a figure of the intellectual of a kind that no longer rises up from popular spontaneity, in the Nietzschean or Foucaultian sense of the plebs, nor from the consciousness of an avant-garde illuminating what remains of the proletariat. These debates between Lenin and Nietzsche, if I can summarize them this way – or more humbly between Lenin and the trade unions – even if crucial, are no longer theoretically creative. As the unresolved problems in scientific practice end up being left behind, these debates have lost their fecundity.

PP: *The conditions are not always wrong! If, tomorrow, anti-Semitism was on the rise, if tomorrow a party of people strayed into authoritarian adventurism, it would be necessary to react, wouldn't it?*

FL: It is already happening . . . As regards the conditions they are never wrong . . . But we would be wrong, ourselves, to take the situation's moments of dreaming or frivolity at face value. We do not have to dream with the situation.

PP: *Explain that. There are countries where frivolity is not appropriate . . .*

FL: There is always an initial or final moment, though often a fantastical one, of frivolity, of peace and utopia in any such situation. But we suspect it is not the only one . . .

PP: *How do you establish the genealogy of the intellectual function?*

FL: It cannot be a historical genealogy. That would be a genealogy in the Nietzschean manner. Given philosophy's historico-systematic, and not simply "structuralist," structure, the first being the much larger horizon possible for Greek presuppositions of thought beyond particular systems, the philosopher tries to coincide with this structure which he puts back into play globally, but expressly so. The traditional intellectual coincides with an abstract moment of this structure in order to carry it to the absolute without the mediations required by the very functioning of this structure. He draws from it effects of incompleteness and segmentation, of "topicality" [*actualité*], with regard for the history that he lives within, so he grounds himself on a particularly abstract concept of the situation.

PP: *This genealogy, do you take it up to the media-friendly intellectual [*intellectuel médiatique*] whom you have denounced elsewhere?*

FL: Whether he ignores it, forgets it, or pretends to ignore it, philosophy, understood in the broader sense, determines with its invariants this media-friendly intellectual. Its fundamental schemes, be they overdetermined by the left–right parliamentary spectrum of contemporary intellectuals, remain effective constraints. It seems to me more and more – even if some cynics already knew it and if the news came to me somewhat late – that the original philosophical posture comes up also with a possible way out, culminating with the media-friendly as a system of intellectual representation. The becoming-world of philosophy, the becoming-philosophy of the world, as the young Marx would say? The truth of the moment, the only one that counts because it constitutes a symptom, is the becoming-mediatized of philosophy and a certain becoming-philosophy of the mediatized. And in this metamorphosis, philosophy very much remains itself. The becoming-system has sustained this branching-off [*ramification*]. One could be thrilled with this mediatized decline of philosophy and mock its ideas of heroic grandeur, but this sort of judgment is never very good. And since it is hardly the Atlantic's fault . . .

PP: *When, for example, you read an article in* Le Monde *or other newspapers about intellectuals and war, in Kosovo or in Iraq, how do you react?*

FL: Pathetic and tragic. I am referring to the intellectuals in their newspaper articles. Pathetic because their reactions always end in their taking a side for one position or for another, or in the search for some small mediation, of some small provisional peace between fierce adversaries and always hiding a thought behind a thought. Tragic because, on the other hand, with them we come to a point of indecision. As a citizen, meaning a network of decisions managed by the State and its subsets, this second aspect is dominant for me. I am torn between all the opinions, and I do not get it: how are the intellectuals able to choose and, apparently without much remorse, pick their side? Being torn between the multiplicity of opinions is of course an untenable position. Opinion, we say, is divided, but it is a poor division which justifies [*fonde*] a consensus for hatred or vengeance. With what concerns the World or history, I hold onto Leibniz's profession of faith, "My great principle, as regards natural things, is that of Harlequin, Emperor of the Moon, [. . .] *that it is always and everywhere in all things just like here*. That is, that nature is fundamentally uniform, although it varies as to more and less."[3] The intellectuals' action can hardly overcome this surface-level variety and touch the bottom. The impossibility of decision is no longer only a psychological problem, it has become a "metaphysical" problem, maybe the modern or contemporary form of anxiety. Non-Philosophy's goal is an "inverting" through a radical inversion of this double and unique logic. Only fidelity still has some meaning

---

[3] G. W. F Leibniz, *New Essays on Human Understanding*, edited by Peter Remnant and Jonathan Bennett (Cambridge: Cambridge University Press, 1996), p. lxvi.

but a fidelity of-the-last-instance, a fidelity which has value as an ultimatum.

PP: *Being torn, doesn't that inevitably lead to a kind of indifferent settling?*

FL: You are going to tell me that adding one's opinion to those of the others undoubtedly forms the life of the World, that it is necessary and responsible, and there are even some philosophers to justify these molecular interventions, these little events, a signature, a speech, or that half-action that a million signatures add up to. Agreed, the philosophers and psychiatrists have proven my case, that of the obsessional, and have offered him remedies, the small imperceptible perception, the clinamen, inclination, consciousness as hesitation, but also the dialectic so he can come together with his adversary but at a "higher" level ... That's enough! The *dissimulitudo of the World* is more and more evident, and so more and more unbearable. What do we make of this awareness, of this very old and very new demand? Indifferent to war? Yes. Indifferent to the peace, which is not the other side of war? No.

PP: *What would such a clear choice as you want mean? Are you erring towards idealism? The intellectuals beg to be in the midst of it all, how would you stay outside of the fray while determining a new function?*

FL: Being in the midst of the fray, but starting off with verbal values, like humanism? The dominant intellectuals scarcely suspect that they will bring about effects, effects of a reticular nature, different from those that they proposed to do or saw themselves doing; they relay exploitation and universalize it in struggling locally against it – this appearance is their true object. How is this practice alone satisfying and how dare it be given an absolute value? This is how I would define the problem more succinctly. Philosophy is only a superior form of the system of opinion. Hence the necessity of moving to a practice, what I call a pragmatics of philosophical opinion, based upon principles other than the principles of philosophy.

PP: *Isn't this project [plan], one that is more sure than the project of opinion, then a project of decision which, if I understand correctly, is not philosophical? It is a subjective decision which cannot be recuperated by philosophical apparatuses. Is it that there is a moment of decision which escapes the logic of history as it is addressed by current such logics? Is that it?*

FL: Yes, but it is more than a moment of philosophical decision, it is a new kind of decision determined by the Name-of-Man, a decision I call non-decisional (of) itself. I am no longer the philosopher who says "we philosophers" and sees the meaning of history while others are exhausting themselves with opinion and with making history. It's not that I critique the necessary opinion and that I want to "get out" and think differently [*autrement*]. Philosophical decision extends opinion right up to an impossible decision, an undecidable decision that in a certain manner fails. But the decision which is non-decisional (of) itself is *for* opinions insofar as it is radically (and not absolutely) heterogeneous to them and comes (from) the future, as Other than philosophical opinions.

PP: *This point of indecision is thought by philosophy as well. Philosophy is very capable of reworking this point of indecision and even in making it a weapon for the subject.*

FL: I absolutely agree, but the problem is that of the relation between decision and the point of indecision! In philosophy, this relation is necessarily continuous or closely related despite every rupture, despite the differences in terms of the levels of reality that one may set between the instance of decision and this point of indecision, whether it is the Other or whether it is neutral regarding the serene unity of the battle of opposites as in Heidegger. There is always a point of serenity, so of indecision and abandonment of duality, but this point of indecision is in continuity with decision. It is as if there were a recto and a verso. The point of indecision is never radical within philosophy. My problem is one of positing a point of radical indecision or not cutting into it with different kinds of philosophical decisions. On the other hand, this point of radical indecision is going to determine them. This is the point of the Undecided rather than of indecision, which I am going to call the Victim-in-person, not the Victim as absolute, because she no longer comes from the absolute, but comes from what I call the radical or the Real. The Victim is no longer debatable or contestable, no longer taboo, yet this is what will come to determine a subject capable of driving philosophy.

PP: *I agree. So let's return now to the example of Iraq. Once you have noted the multiplicity of opinions, can you make out your point of radical indecision?*

---

FL: You want me to commit and give you my "opinions" about certain fiery events and about the intellectuals who are giving fiery performances? Well no, my "opinion" about the war, it is exactly what I am giving you here, in saying what I say and doing what I do, it is a performative action right in the situation. As for the rest, it's enough that, like everyone, I pick up a copy of *Le Monde*, and I will have all possible opinions available, those on paper and on screen, and even my own! I have not repeated the work that others have done better and that I would not be able to do. Dominant intellectuals and philosophers do not do the same job, so when it concerns non-philosophers ... As to the point of radical indecision, the presupposed that I have spoken about, it is certainly not situated in Iraq. It is not situated geo-strategically. It is a "utopian" Real, but it is in this ultimately lived experience [*vécu*] and through it that we receive this war. Demanding a lived experience that is immanent and separated from space and time is the entire problem of the figure and status of the Victim that I am trying to transform. Man is not a victimizable being, he is only such as a subject, but he alone can determine an intellectual *for* the relations of the Victim and history. This Victim is not a represented victim, so it is not her sensible representation or her ideal representation, a Victim in herself as certain philosophers would dream of her. Her positivity resides and is exhausted within her ability to "identify" these representations without reuniting them within a system. This ability to determine maintains the place of its definition. You are asking me to give a definition of what I as a non-philosopher should be thinking about a recent war, but non-philosophy is a practice which excludes definitions, immediate, univocal, and definitive characterizations – too bad for the war, the "genuine" [*vrai*] war and the war of the intellectuals. There are multiple opinions concerning a war, it is a triviality unceasingly proving the intellectuals right. The problem is one of making some use out of these opinions, so that they are all transformed and put to service for the Man within the victim.

PP: *You often say that the philosophers, even those who are critical of historicism – and they are legion – have not said goodbye completely to the philosophies of history. Does non-philosophy constitute a real goodbye to those philosophies of history?*

FL: In principle or in intention, yes. Non-Philosophy is a kind of posture that seems to say goodbye to the World and so also to history, to philosophy, and so on. How is this not running away? In reality this goodbye, or rather this "see you again," is for us inspired by the future which is the mode of Man-in-person's manifestation – meaning that Man is fundamentally an inspired identity, an immanent future. We do not run away, we have always been somewhere other than where we came from, we come from nowhere. To say goodbye is to say see you again and it is finally to say hello for the first time, it is to be capable of maintaining a new relation to the World and to all its attributes, power relations, relations of sexuality, language relations, to that mass of opinions which is the turbulent ocean of the World. The human subject is the New-Born above all!

PP: *What precisely is this posture? Is it a decision of thought at the start? Or does it even have a place to start from?*

FL: There is always a place to start within philosophy itself. But I can't base the whole of my fixed course on this position or this starting point. Non-Philosophy's true structure is what I call unilateral duality. It signifies that there is an aspect which comes from philosophy in any case, and so a starting point within it and a progression, a discussion and some argumentation between opinions. But there is another side which is no longer definable, which does not have its starting point within philosophy, or even within thought. This radical aspect is no longer able to be located and is what I call – in those texts oriented towards mysticism especially – an unlearned knowing, a properly human knowledge (philosophy exceeds man, science ignores the subject). It is a little like a transformation of Rousseau's thesis: man, as Man-in-person, has no fundamental need for scholars and philosophers. However, I am not giving man over to pure sentiment and subjectivity here because I also distinguish the Name-of-Man and the Stranger-subject, as we have said.

PP: *So can you be more specific by contrasting the typical traits of the dominant intellectual?*

FL: This intellectual's style of action is to analyze, to separate, to elucidate, to dissolve the ambiguities, to "bring," as he says, "the truth out into the open" [*faire éclater*], to anonymously demand with values in capital letters, to be at best a transcendental journalist, meaning one devoted to the World, when one is not at worst a "transcendent" journalist, meaning devoted to his daydreams. He claims to conceive this activity as an additional positive force, an action suited to his means, but modest and necessary. Another characteristic is that he needs to inscribe his action within a public space and time expanded under the form of a whole production. He feels the need to make some exhibition, to set up a stage, if not a shop window, for his intervention. One of his dominant traits is that he considers existence to be like a theatre, which comes to him from the farthest ends of philosophy; this is not simply an irritated reaction to this camera-ready show. This intellectual is still related to or close to the philosopher looked upon like a demigod who contemplates the comedy of existence and who laughs – of course he laughs silently because he is defending himself from being cynical, but he still laughs at this spectacle of man's misfortune. On this point Foucault, a good Nietzschean philosopher, gave the game away. Nausea is inevitable here – existence as theatre and entertainment! Did Rousseau deliver his condemnation of the theatre due to these genuine reasons, those of the philosophical lifestyle?

PP: *Why is there this need to inscribe the action of our intellectual in public space, turning that space into a production and exhibition?*

FL: If he wants to intervene in currents events, which I think determines him, these current events force his hand, he is already, *a priori*, inscribed within space and within time. Moreover, in so far as his mode of action is based essentially on division, which in philosophical terms means upon transcendence, he is in an exterior position. He watches the situations, he judges them – of course, you are going to ask me what more could you want or imagine? Even if this is so that he can take a side, he looks down on them and oversees them. This transcendent relation to things forms how he contemplates victims, even if he takes a side in favor of these victims. But this is precisely taking a side in favor of . . ., which is also to contemplate and to watch. It is very important that the intellectual watch, that he contemplate existence in the manner of some great theatre. He perhaps participates in the present and in history, but he also protects himself from human suffering. The pronounced taste for the mediatized comes to him from afar. A psychoanalysis of the theatre of intellectuals would be necessary here . . .

PP: *On top of this dramatization [*théâtralisation*] he fulfils a function of mediation which is today everywhere at work.*

FL: This function of mediation is structural and responds to a restrictive law of the philosophical gesture, but under a reduced or empirical form here. The intellectual does not have at his disposal the enjoyment [*jouissance*] of the system's beautiful unity, which we have talked about. He can only live within separation and in a state of conflict [*conflictualité*]. It is fine to look for some mediation or a form of unification of positions, but this will no longer be the great Hegelian mediation which resolves all contradictions and gives meaning to all historical determinations, it will be an extra small mediation or one that acts like a stopgap. Should we go so far as speaking of an emergency-room intellectual? Or, in any case, a therapeutic intellectual? But the intellectual's task, in the image of a pure psychoanalyst, is not to cure the ills of society, his task is to record them and redistribute them – a redistribution of evil. There is a mediation which is derived from Hegel, but there are also mediators of all kinds who little by little take the place of the Holy Spirit's divine mediation as soon as intellectual action proves to be impossible or sterile. These mediators are not even philosophers but distant figures of the philosopher that are in danger of being wiped out. And philosophy becomes, little by little, this figure that is self-dissipating within the virulence of current events.

PP: *And the humanitarian intellectual? What distinguishes him from the dominant intellectual?*

FL: Is the humanitarian intellectual the new kind of intellectual for the contemporary age? A substitute for the humanist form of intellectual? A cousin on some other branch of their genealogical tree? The intellectual's consciousness has taken on new dimensions or a new tint with the competition of humanitarian organizations and the kind of work they refer to. There was a beginning to the fusion of these roles. This gets into the sense of a universalization of that function which brings assistance to victims or helps troubled groups. Moreover we could ask if this is not a way of looking at the creation of non-governmental intellectual organizations. We could imagine, amongst all the futures that may appear, something of this kind. This would confront that idea that there is a *function of intellectual management for possible decisions*, which intersects with other survival or welfare functions. Maybe the intellectual's function, moving through the interactivity of debate, is a survival function or welfare function for certain groups. Consequently, circumstances are no more conflictual and specific than they have been. Personally, I would want to call the dominant intellectual a "humanitarian" insofar as he necessarily maintains or keeps some final relation to man such as philosophy knows man and so which is not the Name-of-Man.

PP: *Sartre said that, when facing an infant dying of hunger,* Nausea *doesn't measure up. What do you consider the function of the humanitarian intellectual to be with regard to the survival of other people?*

FL: Excuse me, but I can no longer stand these sorts of examples; the phenomenologists did not deprive themselves of these sorts of examples. I find them to be an overwhelming and intimidating abstraction, almost a sin against children and against literature. That said – or refusing to say it – and if something else needs to be said, like it or not survival has become an important humanitarian category for our various societies. From this, we can end up disgusted with this universal obsession with survival, or, on the contrary, we can help this example on so as to give birth to a new ethical consciousness. But the most beautiful ethics are worth what they are normally worth, brandished all the more as they are ridiculed. Survival can also set in motion the problem of the redefinition of the Victim, and so too of justice. But I prefer to follow another path, non-humanitarian but under the sign of the Name-of-Man, so as to try out this definition and, as always, recognize that there are only impossible definitions of the Victim.

PP: *What becomes of pity? What becomes of the order of charity? Isn't there a hierarchy of orders? Isn't bringing some relief better than being offensive?*

FL: When it is a question about man, I find that the orders are disordered. Pity and charity are the limit figures for the humanitarian, they begin to overcome the possibilities of philosophy, from one side to the other they are of the philosophical sphere, for my part I understand pity better than charity, but that just reflects my own insufficiencies. I do not confuse them with the world humanitarian order, whose critique is easier, as it has itself developed its own criticism at the same time as its possibilities. Like every kind of organization and every institution, it has demonstrated its own weaknesses and compromised principles, but only to better survive them, and rightly so. Things do not always happen that way within history. The problem is that of trying to invent all at once a critique of the humanitarian, one which would no longer simply be an auto-critique, and a usage which does not replace the humanitarian, but which is a pragmatics determined otherwise. What I call non-philosophy does not replace those philosophies of the event or other kinds of philosophy, but adds itself to them as a supplementary dimension or another theoretical and practical perspective [*regard*] on their activity.

PP: *Why have those who have wanted to leave philosophy always been tempted by the experience of holiness* [sainteté], *in the broad sense of the term?*

FL: Well, because we cannot leave philosophy except in this way, or even by the way of the artist, or even still by the way, not of the positive scientist like a technician or laboratory worker, but of the mathematician. We can only exit philosophy by "going higher" [*par le haut*]. And holiness, well that is leaving philosophy by . . . the Most-High [*Très-Haut*], albeit made human. What is strange about philosophy is that this discipline does not permeate concrete experiences and concrete practices, but it does touch all of them in mistakenly believing to permeate them. It is close to holiness, to mysticism, to science, to art, but it is not art, not science, not mysticism. It is a well-ordered and transcendental form of opinion, it divides everything, but it has nothing of its own except the more or less formal gesture of reappropriating these experiences. This mode of investment (which provides the type for the dominant intellectual) is a mirage, it is a drive to appropriate which resolves itself in an interminable reappropriation of itself, a skimming off the top of experience by thought but which creates nothing but an allusion to these experiences. Philosophy is the passion necessary for this semblance, of what there is more purely within appearance. The intellectual moves within the philosophical appearance but without the premises of appearance, within a double abstraction that I call "Reality with a Capital-R" [*la-réalité*]. That does not mean that either this or its action are on the level of a subjective mirage or an illusion of perception. As to the determined intellectual, what determines him if not the being-separated or holiness of the Human Real?

# The Victim and the Understanding of Crime

PP: *In* Future Christ *you write: "Heresy does not know the 'memorially correct' or its contrary, without which it is a question of denying the watchful pitched against one another. Under whatever perspective it is, as long as it is not that of scientific or ethical corruption and racist ulterior motives, we have never been interested in minimizing crime or suffering, in dissolving them in the always too vast geo- and historico-political 'considerations', to say nothing of the philosophical generalizations [. . .] that challenge the subject's range of suffering and misfortune."*[1] *I suggest that you move on now to this central theme of the Victim, in relation with philosophy. Then we will see what the Victim is in non-philosophy. What can philosophy say about the Victim?*

FL: There is a philosophical paradox regarding the Victim. On the one hand, philosophy has almost nothing

---

[1] François Laruelle, *Future Christ: A Lesson in Heresy*, trans. Anthony Paul Smith (New York and London: Continuum, 2010), p. 95.

to say about her. We could say at the very least that the Victim is not one of philosophy's favorite themes. Sometimes an allusion is made on the basis of other themes, justice in particular or war, but the Victim is a kind of zero point or blind spot for philosophy. In contrast, which is the other side of the paradox, it is possible to project a philosophical image of the Victim and that is what I am going to attempt. Structural or conceptual projections are possible. In a general way, within an ontological representation of the Victim, she is only originally present with some distance, a distance I will call *victomological distance*. A victim can necessarily only show herself under every form of representation from somewhere else, media-friendly ones as well as conceptual ones, with a certain objectified distance. Even when she seems given in some very immediate way as in the case of television images, the Victim is, in reality, given across a distance, that of the image. This distance is the mark of philosophy and the cause of a certain disinterest regarding the Victim. The image alludes to everything by creating the impression of giving the Victim in flesh and blood.

PP: *In the* Discourse on Inequality, *when Rousseau speaks about pity as spontaneous action, one is within the language of the heart, of the immediate. Rousseauian compassion is absolutely without distance from the point of view of the sensible. Isn't the distance that you are talking about uniquely a sensible distance?*

FL: Even in the most immediately apparent pity there is still some distance. The Victim has to show herself under the form of another person, even if it is another person with whom we have some sensible contact and who is immediately affective. Affectivity clashes with rationality or rationalization, but it does not clash with victimological distance. The Victim is given in ekstasis, albeit one that is sometimes forgotten.

PP: *But what then is the structure of victimological distance?*

FL: It is not a simple distance, able to be measured empirically or geometrically. It has a double dimension, two kinds of ekstasis and not a single one. The first kind of distance belongs to what I could call the "laid-out Victim" [*la victime couchée*], but laid flat next to the nudity of history, on the ground of time and space, and this is not a metaphor, this is the Victim given horizontally, under her most intuitive form. And then there is another dimension of the Victim, this is the Victim that I will call the "standing" or vertical Victim – so, for example, the crucified Victim – this is Christ as the exemplary victim, abased but still standing. So there are two kinds of transcendence for the victim, a double and unique ekstasis, the syntagmatic or horizontal dimension and the paradigmatic or prototypical dimension. For the Victim, there is some multiplicity or other, as well as a prototype.

PP: *What side is the kamikaze on?*

FL: It seems to me that he resembles two figures at the same time, since he sacrifices himself for a god or God. The kamikaze was the individual who assumed his absolute responsibility for the emperor. The ground of history is covered with victims but there is an exemplary victim, unique each time, who is charged with binding the body of the people or humanity – this is the high Victim, who is transcendent and gathers together. The Victim constitutes mediation between the divine and human by paying tribute to the latter. Christ is this inevitably double Victim, at once within history – that is, Christ as a human, abased and suffering – and at the same time the redeemer of humanity. To return to the kamikaze, he functions within a context that is also religious, but the transcendence of the kamikaze is more radical than that of Christ. Christ is both more divine and more human than the kamikaze, an ordinary person who is marked right away by the emperor's seal and who leaves his people in order to be trained for his sacrifice. Both are chosen and both are saviors, but Christ's election is made according to universal humanity, while the election of the kamikaze is decided by the sovereign, by a people, or by a faith. And, as a result, given this limitation of humanity to a single faithful people or a single nation, the transcendence of this relation to salvation is still more radical than within Christianity. In fact, for Christians, it is the martyrs who more closely resemble the kamikazes. Needless to say, I would like to rid thought of this sacrificial image of the Victim, which is just the religious image or representation created by the victors. It is the cynical generosity of those who triumph which gives some meaning to the death of victims. I believe that we should not paint victims in a more compassionate image, but instead abandon every image and attribute to them a powerlessness which transforms the victors. We could wonder if every victim, even involuntarily, is not sacrificial: I mean that these piles of bodies, mass graves, and funeral pyres serve to unify groups, indeed even humanity and a history. This law of the history-world, apparently unknown to the dominant intellectual in his narrowness, will be material for the determined intellectual.

PP: *Isn't there a danger in pushing the Victim to the front so much?*

FL: I believe that it is instead necessary to finally place the Victim in her true non-philosophical place. A danger lies in wait for the victims, of course, but not always where we think the danger lies. It is philosophy or the World that reappropriates victims and inscribes them within their viciously circular logic. Moreover, once inside this circle, this Victim changes her status. She is only innocent at the moment she is killed, exterminated, but she is not innocent if we relate her to the global and worldly cycle of violence. It is a very general schema which includes the Victim twice within the cycle of violence. Within this circle, every victim becomes in turn a persecutor in relation to all other possible victims. And every persecutor in turn is a victim of another persecutor. It is a terrible idea but this is an idea traced by philosophy. The more this relation between the Victim and the persecutor sprawls across the plane of history and sticks to the plane of history and to universal becoming, the more chance there is that the Victim will find herself in the persecuting role or of being a former persecutor. The paradigmatic dimension tends to erase itself in the syntagmatic or horizontal dimension, but it subsists as a monstrous body of history and the State-world which falls back upon the victims . . .

PP: *This is very dangerous. For example, can we say that the former victims of the camps have become Israeli persecutors? Is that an untenable statement?*

FL: It is entirely tenable, but what kind of necessity does it have? Primo Levi's remark does not apply only to the camps. It is a philosophical and universal law that is inherited, like memory, from the preceding generation. I have even said that it was possibly planned by a perfected Western philosophy. Within the greatest disjunction, within the greatest difference, there will be some affinity between the Victim and executioner, the tortured and the torturer, etc. This is a universal scheme that allows us to understand, at least provisionally, certain relations of force or events within history. That this should be considered a particularly dangerous formula for Israel, I entirely believe, but because Judaism has a totally different reading of history from the one that we find in Greek philosophy. Judaism thinks history as a contretemps of the relation of the chosen people to God, their persecutor. This relationship of infinite transcendence does not end in a totalization of victims and persecutors, a totalization which is eminently Greek and which implies a kind of reciprocal approximation of the Victim or executioner. This proximity is a problem that the philosophers are unable not to put forward. I think that Sartre has put it forward through the gaze. The gaze, but not only the gaze, is a mode of victimological distance.

PP: *But, from this law of the persecuted Victim, could the violence exercised against the Victim be made legitimate?*

FL: Of course, it is continuously made legitimate, and by the intellectuals themselves! There are plenty of intellectuals, jurists, doctors, politicians, and philosophers who can find causes and draw out sufficient reasons for them. Every scenario is possible and so tempting for the intellectuals. Two extreme scenarios from this circle appear in reality. Either, effectively, any violence can always be made legitimate, we are not going to start discriminating between true or bad forms of legitimation, legal reasons and twisted rationalizations. This philosophical possibility has, at any rate, a few symptoms in historical reality. It is philosophically legitimate and necessary to find some sufficient reason for violence – only philosophers locked away in their system can believe in the exceptions that they imagine and only they can believe in their logodicy.[2] Only reasons of the State can call forth legitimate violence. Or, on the contrary, we can refuse and condemn entirely [*globalement*] this circle of violence and call for a universal pity, a circle of pity. These are the non-Hegelian philosophies, of the Rousseauian or Schopenhauerian kind; they refuse reason within history, but such a pity is still universal and responds to the philosophical criteria of the system under a concealed form.

We could add, in this context and from this interpretation (which is precisely the object to be transformed), that the Victim is a kind of pretender in Plato's sense, a pretender to the truth and above all to justice. This

---

[2] Laruelle here is punning on "theodicy," or arguments attempting to justify suffering or the existence of evil in the World. Leibniz's conception of sufficient reason figured in his classic formulation of theodicy. Here Laruelle has simply replaced the figure of God (*theos*) with that of the Greek philosophical *logos*. [Translator's note.]

pretension, which is at once the law and the desire of the right to justice, strangely recalls the philosophical gesture. There is a kind of homology, or in any case an affinity, between the Victim and the philosopher: the Victim being the dark side, hidden, of the philosopher, his unthinkable verso. The unexpected meeting of phi-losophy and Christianity would be a symptom of this, as Nietzsche suggested. Of course, the philosopher does not look like a victim at all. He appears, on the contrary, just like a hero, driven by the hope of triumph. A point here about method, and an explanation: I am forming rather different, rather multiple, interpretative hypotheses about the Victim and the intellectual. I am not, in fact, describing these situations in a general way, I am brack-eting history as the fact of facts, and so I am describing its structures, its possible projections, and finally I am going to set up a kind of utopia with non-philosophy – a utopia of the Victim and of the intellectual that is grounded upon a refusal of justification through history. I believe that this method – that of the worst – is the only method that still remains available for us if we are to hope for a salvation and not identify ourselves with the unfathomable psychology of dictators and tyrants. We have not yet explored all the possibilities of thought, and so all the possibilities of struggle. I form this hypothesis of the worst, but under human conditions, so as not to sink into the worst of the worst.

PP: *What strikes me is that all the current intellectual discussions on these kinds of problems are discussions so limited in their horizon – so determined by that his-torical, political, indeed mediatized, contingency – that they become useless.*

FL: It's an obvious fact that we are more or less sensitive to, but when we are very sensitive, we are tempted either to free ourselves from the intellectuals' differend by taking refuge, not within philosophy, but within the more limited and more solid forms of knowledge. Or we are tempted to make the leap into the non-philosophical type of thought. The determined intellectual lets himself be motivated by, but not determined by, history. He only finds occasions or contingencies that allow him, not to think the Victim, but to do "victim thinking" [*penser victime*].[3] The great difference between the dominant intellectual and the determined intellectual lies here, thinking the victim or victim thinking. Despite a few efforts – Rousseau's in particular – the Victim is most often a victimological object, an alibi for the intellectual, good for justifying the abandonment of all conceptual rigor, for demanding affectivity, sensitivity, alterity, etc. Philosophy has its victim, but the Victim of philosophy is perhaps the repression of another victim, too obvious to not be forgotten or unnoticed.

PP: *I would like to ask you a question taken from Alain Badiou's* Ethics, *on the survivors of the camps. He writes that: "this is always achieved precisely through enormous effort, an effort acknowledged by witnesses [. . .] as an almost incomprehensible resistance on the*

---

[3] This locution shares many of the same difficulties found in translating Luce Irigaray's *parler femme*. Laruelle's *penser victime* could be translated in a number of different ways, as could Irigaray's formulation, which has led her translators to leave *parler femme* untranslated. However, as this isn't a phrase which recurs throughout Laruelle's work, I have chosen to translate it as "victim thinking," though it could have also been translated "to think victim," meaning something close to thinking as a victim but without the sense of distance implied in the "as." [Translator's note.]

*part of that which, in them, does not coincide with the identity of the victim. This is where we are to find Man, if we are determined to* think *him: in what ensures, as Varlam Shalamov puts it in his* Stories of Life in the Camps, *that we are dealing with an animal whose resistance, unlike that of a horse, lies not in his fragile body but in his stubborn determination to remain what he is – that is to say, precisely something other than a victim, other than a being-for-death, and thus:* something other than a mortal being. "[4] *After this he develops the theme of man's singularity as immortal.*

FL: From my point of view, this is the boasting of a philosopher who is expressing a beautiful assurance. A simple question though: is the Victim comparable – *this was what Badiou contrasted the victim with* – is the Victim comparable to a beast? The entire problem is in the formula "the identity of the victim." Wouldn't our philosophy tend to confuse the identity of the Victim with the state of a beast in order to better compare the Victim to the immortal state? To reduce man to the apparatus of death and immortality? The reduction of man to the subject and to predicates again and again. This comes from the renewal of philosophy and, as a result, renews philosophy's terrible definition of man, a political animal, a religious animal, a speaking animal, etc. Here we have the new man of philosophy, an immortal animal! He is not sure that the Victim will always be reduced to the state of a beast, particularly when he is murdered, and even when he is tortured,

---

[4] Alain Badiou, *Ethics: An Essay on the Understanding of Evil*, trans. Peter Hallward (London and New York: Verso, 2001), pp. 11–12.

unless he let himself be taken away by literary over-excitement afterward. This is a traditional concept, wherein man is defined as a philosophizing animal, an animal superior to his becoming-victim but who remains an animal. The identity of the Victim absolutely does not amount to this natural or bestial state. I think that this sort of particularly exciting formula – and I do recognize that excitement – for the grandeur of man and his heroism is what we now would have to try and overcome or understand differently.

Man is reduced *to the state* of a beast, or some other state, but is this state a predicate and does the predicate make the man, or at least Man-in-person? Does he have a "victim identity," a being-victim as a new predicate? In our desire to give man a more elevated predicate than that of the beast, we are entering once again into the war of predicates. Philosophy, police officer of the predicates! "Victim, show me your papers and prove your state!"

PP: *You seem to say that the distinction between the animal and the immortal singularity of man is a way of boldly drawing the line of demarcation between the Victim and the resister. Would the Victim become an animal and would the resister become someone who would resist animalization?*

FL: This seems to me to condemn any attempt to take the Victim seriously. I do not posit a duality of Victim and resister. That is a split which still calls for an ultimate synthesis carried out by heroism. In this synthesis, the resister can be a victim, but he rises above this state. But there is still another problem. We have to understand

Shalamov's formulation from within its context, this is someone who is a true witness to the camps and who is not at all in the position of the philosopher reading the testimony of the witness. I am taking the liberty of making a fundamental difference between Badiou and Shalamov, as Hegel makes a difference – unfortunately to finally negate it – between "we philosophers" and the phenomenological consciousness that is engaged within struggle, within labor, within suffering and who, as such, has a right to take up these discourses of resistance, fidelity, and obstinacy. I am very ill at ease when philosophy takes charge of the witness' discourse and makes a philosophy out of it. I recognize this is a violent enough critique, but one or two years after the publication of Badiou's *Ethics*, I published *Ethique de l'Étranger*[5] and in there is a reflection on the Victim that of course comes out of a completely different position. I do not want to be a philosopher of the Victim, either to praise the Victim or to "revise" her and critique the "ideology of victimhood."

PP: *This is not very philosophical or technical, but it is taken in a very media-friendly direction by someone like Alain Finkelkraut. The idea he advanced, in order to get past Sartre and Marxism, is that the story was easy in the age of the dialectic since there were the oppressors and the oppressed. Today, by contrast, it is much more complex. All the anti-totalitarians today tell us that, on the whole, we have gone through a dark period of Manichaeism – which remains to be seen if we read*

---

[5] François Laruelle, *Ethique de l'Étranger: Du Crime contre l'humanité* (Paris: Kimé, 2000).

*Sartre attentively – and that we are returning to an era of complexity, of responsibility, of a renewal of morality, hence the revival of Camus who somewhat prepared the way for the moral intellectual of today. What do you think of this idea of the sixties, the dialectical years, having been a period of total Manichaeism that we are now leaving?*

FL: It was the age of Communism as much as of the dialectic. That depends of course on what we mean by a dialectic, which is more subtle. Effectively we have left this "Manichaeism" (what a disgrace that this philosopheme has been kidnapped by the most vulgar discourse!) but by coming into something worse, into "complexity," which is simply the combination of complicity and hand-wringing, and its parousia. This era of complexity has only made known or made credible the principle of the circle of persecution. The themes of persecution, of the hostage, of extermination are not really Marxist themes but themes with a much more recent origin, both Jewish and anti-totalitarian.

So as to add some nuance to what has been said, this is a *hypothesis about the meaning of history*, which unties some knots, which allows certain political, ethnic, and social relations to be formalized, but which cannot be applied in an absolute way. History cannot be totally absorbed by this schema because that would mean that the World is becoming philosophy in full, as Marx said, or that philosophy is becoming a world. But that is not at all what happens locally, knowing that there are pockets of resistance and transcendence in relation to this schema, pockets which are precisely represented, in particular, by a certain

Judaism and also by what we sometimes call back to – gnosis – which we understand constitutes a theoretical cuss-word. We can change the Victim into a persecutor and the persecutor into a victim; it is, locally, very easy. But I would refuse this hypothesis as a universal empirical law of history because it seems to me to be too overwhelmingly philosophical to exhaust everything that happens.

PP: *That said, we no longer have a choice as easy as in the age of Communism or the dialectic, because the dialectic was still very solid from this point of view.*

FL: The problem is that all these relations have become metastable. So, yes, it is necessary to complicate our ethics in turn. However, we do not fight against complexity by using a complexity of the same kind or at the same level. It is not about passing from the complexity of all-responsibility, and from the charge that has become a recrimination, to another practice which would be one of invention or of the imagination. Only the introduction of ethics itself into utopia (since utopia is the yeast of imagination) may put salvation back within the reach of humanity. And then we can stop confusing Communism with a radical concept of utopia. Philosophical utopias and the camps are models of each other, that is not what I am looking for.

PP: *I was very struck, this winter, by the vision of this young man in the streets of Moscow whose friend lay dead next to him. He said, "for now, I am resisting." Can this point of survival escape philosophical recapture? Does it have to fall under solidarity, politics?*

FL: What happens to the Victim who has not had the time or the unlikely courage to resist? Philosophy forgets her, evidently; she does not emerge, she is not interesting. As if we have chosen to be a beast or to be an immortal hero! The philosopher has passion for parousia and speech – either the Victim speaks or it is the philosopher who speaks: the Victim must let out a sigh that the philosopher can inscribe in his system, as Kierkegaard has said, a cry of suffering as a footnote to Hegel's *Science of Logic*! I am tired, may as well admit it, of this theme of resistance that posits that man is an animal who drags himself out of animality, an oppressed person who resists his oppressors, and who consummates himself in philosophical heroism and in the articles of the intellectual. The majority of victims are mute, dead, or reduced to silence there and then in the very moment of the crime; they long ago lost the taste for the ambrosia of *logos*. You understand why I hold that the Victim is a victim twice over. The uninteresting Victim, without a future in the philosopher's work – that Victim interests me even if I am not quite sure how to take her or let myself be taken by her. The true Victim is she who, unlike Socrates, does not leave some monumental image behind her, does not leave some dignified speech to be contemplated by a philosopher.

PP: *What is the status for you of the homeless person who refuses, as is often the case, to be taken care of by the city authorities, or taken into council housing or the projects?*

FL: "We will force them to be free" like Rousseau said, to be inside where it is warm, to be properly fed and, subjected to the benefits of a nearly normal existence, we will force their own survival. This humanitarian forcing (there are other forms, like the forcing of law and order) is rife with contradictory opinions because philosophy provides both for forcing and for not forcing individuals, and that is the absolute forcing which passes over this contradiction of judgment, so at least we can snatch it from those particular opinions that most philosophers and intellectuals cultivate and which are intra- if not infra-philosophical. As for non-philosophy, it clearly accepts in this sort of problematic an initially forced hand (the presupposed Real) and not a final one like philosophy does. But one that is, at the same time, as if void of determination. This is a determining force without determination. Enigmatic? That is what the determined intellectual presupposes.

PP: *Apparently the Victim as you think her is not the Victim that the philosophers reflect on, along with all those who stand upon human misfortune in order to ground some philosophical approach [une pensée philosophique] to the victim. What is the difference then between your Victim-in-person and the philosophers' Victim?*

FL: Apprehended by philosophy, inserted into the circle of persecution, the Victim is known to pass through the medium of representation under all its forms: visual, judicial, military, etc., which are philosophizable. I am trying to distinguish the sufficient, represented Victim, with her two correlated modes of representation, laying down and standing up, and the Victim-in-person who must rather claim to be singular, even though this formula will not be satisfactory. It is the Victim as Human Identity or presupposed Real, not as any "identity" whatsoever or singular case. This "concept" of the Victim-in-person, or rather "first name" because she is no longer a concept, has to make possible a new practice for intellectuals, one which would remove the arrogance [*suffisance*] from its actual practice and would transform it.

PP: *What does it mean when you say that the Victim-in-person is not a represented victim? How do we not imagine a victim, how do we not define her, not characterize her with properties or effects of history?*

FL: The philosophical horizon, meaning the conceptual tradition of representation and its philosophical critique, is implied by the notion of the Victim-in-person. This is a term = X, an empty and abstract symbol "by dint" ["*à force*"] of identity or immanence, but in such a way that it has effects on history because it is abstract and not able to be determined by history. It is as if we had put forward not an empirically verified victim, an object of a true discourse, but a victim-symbol which determines or makes possible a true discourse on victims. There is the true without truth, the true which has not been verified, validated, but which goes on to allow, under a simply axiomatic form, the transformation of the discourse of representation. This is a postulate, but not an ontological postulate full of reason or understanding projected onto history; it is an immanent postulate or, better, a first name for these axioms. We can only represent it by way of an objective appearance and an illusion, but it implies that thought functions otherwise than how it is formed in its mores, its traditional codes and its current ones. Here we can only state the axioms concerning the Just (the Victim) and her effect on justice. The Victim-in-person is not an abstraction of the classical kind. She is one abstract rather than an abstraction.

PP: *Who is the Victim-in-person?*

FL: She is Man-in-person. Man-in-person is liable to several designations, and if we give Man-in-person the designation of Victim-in-person then it is according to the situation and the problem to be treated, which is here the problem of victimization and the role of the intellectuals in comparison to the victims. Man is a zero point within the forms of knowing which rise from non-philosophy, and Man is susceptible to several characterizations – in particular, he is philosophically able to be victimized. We can form several kinds of axioms from concrete themes taken from history, philosophy, situations, but these will be axioms, meaning that they will not have validity only for Man-in-person but effects upon history. The situation, as in Marxism, is decisive, but the situation is what we think Man-in-person with and not what we think Man-in-person through.

PP: *How do you approach the problem of justice?*

FL: We could form secondary axioms and say, for example, that the Victim-in-person is neither just nor unjust but – this is her effect – that she is what suffices to determine a subject *for* and from the mechanisms of justice, philosophy, and representation. Or that the Victim is just before all justification, that there is no need to justify her or to philosophize her. She is, in one sense, the immanent model of justice and not the Platonic one. The Victim is so just that she does not have to be justified within a *Logos*, it is she who *determines a subject (the intellectual) in-the-last-instance for the philosophical contradictions of justice.*

Someone might ask me to give an example of some representation of this Man-in-Man, but this is precisely the point where, by definition, Man-in-person does not represent himself, but the point is also that philosophy tries to represent him. Hence the struggle between Man-in-person and philosophy, between those who will be the Victim-in-person and history as victimization. This is the unknown Victim of the philosophers, or even the Victim that is too well known and so is forgotten by them – it doesn't matter which, the only question is that of knowing what effect of determination she has on history and the constitution of an intellectual subject. She must, as a matter of priority, change the mode of the intellectual's thinking, modify in a more or less radical way his theoretical field and the kind of action that he makes possible.

PP: *What would this action consist of?*

FL: We could begin by eliminating some solutions. Firstly, this is not Platonism, meaning that the Victim-in-person is not the Victim in-itself, an Idea or Model, a paradigm for the Victim. Secondly, this is no longer a concrete victim taken from the field of battle or the television screen. She is no longer the Victim as an Other [*Autrui*], as she can be within a generalized Jewish context; she is not another person [*autrui*] who will be persecuted by me or by the philosophical universal, but no longer is it myself who will be persecuted by another person. So, what is the Victim-in-person? What is the identity of the Victim-in-person, her attributes? This is precisely the question that must be refused as it applies philosophical interrogation to things and to the World. We do not realize that this apparently natural way of thinking is not the most adapted one and it is even a falsifying or repressive way of thinking.

*Who is she?* is a better question because the *who* indicates something like a subjectivity, a singularity, an identity . . . but it remains too deceptive still. In the contemporary context, Nietzschean for example, the question *who* refers to a philosophy of the universal subject-force, there are no longer anything but subjects or subjectivities, actions or subjective passions, of desire, etc. The question could contain some meaning if the Victim was one such subject. As "victim" is one of the possible designations of Man, or a mode of the Name-of-Man, then I am positing that she is not a subject. It is necessary to radically or unilaterally distinguish between Man and the (intellectual) subject. Which does not mean that the subject is inhuman, but it does mean that the subject is not simply human like Man himself.

PP: *But then how do we go forward if we cannot give the Victim a definition?*

FL: A "normal" definition serves to put forward a subject and a set of properties which speaks for the Victim. But as what I call Victim is not of the order of a subject whose properties we could affirm, it will be

necessary, if we want to give the equivalent of a definition, to proceed differently. It will be necessary to say,
for example, that the Victim is who determines, through
her identity, a subject *for* the relations of her representation and her nonrepresentation, and from them. This
kind of definition imposes an asceticism on the passion
for representation since it refuses to lay a hand directly
on the Victim. No one, I assure you, has ever seen, seen
and intuited with their eyes, the Victim-in-person. Is she
subversive? No, she "inverts" common sense but also
philosophical sense. She gives the most radical identity to
the relation such that they are immediately prehensible
within representation. Definitions by way of a subject,
an attribute or a predicate, and in particular that definition of man as resisting animal – from my point of view,
these philosophical definitions are no longer effective.
We have to leave behind these blendings and give pref-
erence to the axiomatic style. The Victim-in-person is
like a concentrated axiom which the intellectuals could
provide themselves with in order to transform their own
action. This provides some indications concerning the
meaning of what I call non-philosophy, which proceeds
through hypotheses or axioms, indeed through utopias,
and which refuses to let itself be locked within the facts,
not in order to deny facts or history, but in order to be
able to explain the philosophical dimension of history.
The axiom is (pre)supposed true and that is enough for
me.

PP: *I imagine that you are not constructing a new theory
of annunciation and that your Victim-in-person is not
some phenomenological remainder, but I would like
to understand how you are able to gesture towards her*

*even if you don't approach her in the literal sense of the term. Is it that you can extract the Victim-in-person from the World and appearance, from ousia and presence, as well as other Greek themes, in order to give her some real content, in the sense that you intend?*

FL: The Victim-in-person is not the object of an annunciation. She is the Announced-in-person who determines the subject as an annunciation, she is the substance of an ultimatum or the future such as it comes. I want to try and make clear the way in which she escapes presence or in which she does not exist. She is what I have called a real presupposed. We must posit her in a practically dogmatic way in order to understand what happens within thought, but this is not a transcendent or metaphysical dogmatism, since she is immanent Man (and not "interior man"). This is language, but language is from thought, even the most long-winded intellectuals think – they simply think about objective appearances. This is not a formal axiomatic; the Real is not a simple word or symbol. We cannot speak of Man and the Victim-in-person except with help, but not in the interior of the dominant intellectual's language, the language of history or politics. It all depends on the usage that we make of thought and language. But in my usage, I designate the Real without constituting it, I designate it without producing it, it is a presupposed.

I am absolutely not saying that every empirical man is a victim, at most they are historically able to be victimized, but that victim-being is in-the-last-instance one lived in-Man. This is not a generalization or a totality. In order to understand the relationship to victims and in order to transform it, so as not to add to their misfortunes with the circle of philosophy, of politics, a thought under the sign of the Name-of-Man is necessary.

PP: *Do you think that philosophy adds to the actual misfortune of victims the belief that this misfortune is definitive? That man is the only necessary Victim in order to think our relation to victims and modify that relation?*

FL: Belief or the refusal of belief – in both cases, the specifically philosophical belief adds to the actual misfortune of victims. The determined intellectual is he who comes to raise this belief to the definitive and sufficient character of the victims' misfortunes. It isn't about believing that we can abolish misfortune, but we can abolish ideological presuppositions, the philosophical ones that besiege the victims. The actual misfortune is of course treated, transformed, at once through history and through the dominant intellectuals who can alleviate this misfortune and accentuate it. But they add, even more, a faith in the constitutive sufficiency of this misfortune, *even when they refuse it*, either they say that all men are victims, or they say that man by definition is not a victim. I refuse this alternative because it is just based on this belief in the sufficiency of philosophy and in the possibility of definitions. This thought is transformed not simply by turning itself towards concrete and historical victims, but in placing itself under the Victim-in-person or the Name-of-Man more generally. We can only regulate the problem of the relationship to victims by presupposing that it is Man, and not the autotherapy of the history-world, which determines this relationship.

---

PP: *I would like it if you developed this theme of belief. Philosophy has moved past the theme of belief in providence, under all its theological forms, to that of belief in the World. I am thinking of Nietzsche. Belief in this world has become consubstantial with every form of historical transcendence. "What should we believe?" is a question which is unable to find any meaning or response in the context of non-philosophy, but is it maybe necessary to pass through a radical atheism, in order to displace the theme of faith and knowledge, as you did in* Future Christ?

FL: There is a place within non-philosophy to treat belief. The idea of belief in the World is a universal idea which does not exist only in the works of Nietzsche and in phenomenology. The phenomenologists, Husserl, Heidegger, Merleau-Ponty, are of course the ones who have best presented the phenomena of belief in the World with the idea of perception as originary faith. I try to understand, with these philosophers, and also with Kant and the transcendental dialectic, this idea that the World, setting aside the content of things and knowledge, of practices, is an objective appearance and a belief, a fundamental belief in the Whole. If there is an element within which it is necessary to replace all the more restrained beliefs, like those beliefs of a theological or mythological order, it is the World as an object of a certain belief. There is a faith in the World which sustains philosophy and functions as a "natural attitude" grounding all our judgments. Philosophy occupies itself not so much with particular objects as with what forms the worldliness of these objects.

PP: *What is the potential treatment for this belief within non-philosophy?*

FL: Non-Philosophy has precisely this belief as an object to be examined. From there non-philosophy operates in two ways. In the first moment it suspends this universal belief in the World, which can just as easily pass through universal history as through certain uses of science; this is the role of the Name-of-Man as presupposed. Then, in the second moment, it in turn explicitly brings back these judgments, which are based upon belief in the World or in history, to the unilateral primacy of Man and to the priority of the Intellectual-subject who follows and constitutes himself out of the World. There is a space for belief outside of itself. Leaving belief in the World by itself is to destroy it under its legislative and authoritarian aspect, all the while conserving it as an object of experience. We abandon the faith specific to the World and its modes not because we are passing over a terrain which, in-itself, is not a terrain of faith, properly speaking. But rather we are given the means of rendering them intelligible and explaining them. More precisely, what I call belief is always a phenomenon of double belief. Believing that there is a single belief is the way belief works [*le fait de croyance*], it is the assurance, the immanent certitude, of every form of belief. Within belief, we believe in belief. Not only do we believe, but we make belief the ultimate foundation of our relation to things. Belief splits itself, there is the belief-object, the belief in things, which is not concerned with destroying but explaining, and there is a second belief which is the belief of the subject in this belief. The mark of philosophy? Twice a victim, twice a belief, etc.

PP: *Does being a victim of interpretation mean being a victim of the conflict of interpretations, the Victim being immediately pulled into a philosophico-worldly circuit? Foucault has spoken about a disciplining of the body and he would have certainly interrogated those psychological units involved when a victim has been designated. Or does the Victim refer to something else?*

FL: Intellectuals are absolutely like everyone else [*tout le monde*], they think within a horizon that, most of the time, they don't display. The greatest horizon, the thought-world or the philosophizability of things, globalizes interpretation. This is what makes every event become at the same time an interpretation that is self-legitimating and self-justifying. So, in pushing this logic to the extreme, we are always a victim twice and never once. Nietzsche and Deleuze already saw the problem: everything in philosophy splits itself. Every empirical phenomenon is accompanied by a globalizing interpretation which comes to reinforce it, legitimate it, and juxtapose some alienating belief to actual alienation. It is this alienation of opinion that the determined intellectual tries to call into question. His role is not to intervene on the ground like the dominant intellectual, but to give rigor and reality to his action, giving him his true object.

PP: *Since this, this belief in the World, concerns effective reality, how can we understand, even better since we have not yet made it understood how your Real is evidently not this reality? It is the same word. If we pass it through Hegelian rationality, we see clearly that your Real presupposes a rationality that is not worldly. But can we clarify these different fields of thought?*

FL: I have already insisted on the duality between the World and the Real, or even Man-in-person, in the radical sense. Reality that is said to be effective is the reality of the World or history such as they appear within the interior of themselves and so as the philosophies think them. Reality is effective because it is a synthesis of facts and ideas, of phenomena and interpretations; it is this synthesis that forms their effectivity. The World's effectivity is, then, of a philosophical kind. What I call the Real is of a completely different nature. It is not based on philosophy or on transcendence, it is radically immanent. So it is what is heterogeneous, by definition, to effective reality. The Real is not effective or does not "exist." It is a necessary but insufficient condition, void of reality, but necessary in order to think effective reality.

PP: *In order to think effective reality? But at the same time you say that the Real is what allows us to think the link between the nameable and unnameable.*

FL: Yes. The link between the nameable and the unnameable, the decidable and the undecidable, the sayable and the ineffable, this link is philosophy itself or the World's reality. Philosophy always forms this link: it always has two aspects or two sides, each referring to the other. What I call the Real is no more decidable than undecidable, nameable than unnameable. We have said it, it determines in-the-last-instance this relation under the form of a subject.

PP: *You say that this is an immediate datum [une donnée immédiate] but at the same time that it is not something*

*we can prove. And at the same time that it would be too
much to say that we receive it, that it happens to us. So
since we are not within the order of certainty or uncer-
tainty, what order are we in?*

FL: It is a proof, but it is a proof which has not been
produced by a test. Or even, it is the lived of life, but
it is not life that has produced this lived. We have to
begin within the lived, in what is already given without
there having been some prior givenness. So, in a certain
way, we begin in the definite without there having been
a definition.

PP: *What order is this given from? Does it have to be an
order of phenomenality?*

FL: It constitutes an order all of its own. We can use
psychoanalysis or even phenomenology in order to give
it a name within axioms. It is a phenomenon but an
immanent one. We don't have to return to the categories
of phenomenology, reception, or givenness. Man does
not even receive his own immanence, nor does he give
himself his immanence as a subject but only as a human.
The immanent lived is this very Man, Man-in-One if we
want to put it that way. And even more, he does not in
reality even receive it, he is it. This is not a radical beginning. The human Real has primacy over the subject,
but it is the subject which is the radical beginning even
though it comes, in a certain way, "after" the Real.

PP: *In Régis Debray's* L'Emprise *there is a chapter entitled, "Y a-t-il encore un réel?" ["Is there still a real?"].
For him the ascendancy [*l'emprise*] of mediatized power*

*is not the ascendancy of some unique thinking but of what*
*he calls the unique world. From there he takes aim at the*
*humanitarian crusades, the vigilance of the politico-moral*
*world which would prevent us from ascending to his-*
*torical and political forms other than those of the rights*
*of man. The duty to interfere becomes the ability to inter-*
*fere with and the means of imposing upon everything an*
*ideology, relayed by intellectual journalists and the new*
*missionaries of rights, making any discussion about the*
*historical Real and every true debate between intellectuals*
*impossible. What do you think about that?*

FL: The World has effectively become still more unique
than it was – that is, it was the thought-world, but it
has become what it was. There is a humanitarian globalization [*globalisation*], a tendency towards an ethical
globalization [*globalisation*], every discussion fits more
and more into this frame. I would also say that reality,
not the Real, is on the way to disappearing. But I would
add that the Real for its part has never been substantial
within the World in the sense that the World has the
form that has been given to it by philosophy. So it is
entirely natural that everything tends to dissolve into
simulacra, or eventually into fantasies, and that we are
always in search of the Real, so that there are now more
philosophers than ever! The whole world has always
looked for the Real. But I think that we have to take
a leap and admit that the Real "is not of this world"
– admit that we will not find it through the means of
history, politics, or philosophy.

This would explain how debates between intellectuals are of the order of a spinning wheel or a double
bind. These debates are structured like a Gordian knot

– arguments on all sides, even when they are apparently opposed face to face, are still united more profoundly and elicit one another. Everyone knows the arguments of their opponent, they have internalized them to various degrees, so that this mutual understanding blocks every truly intellectual decision. The discussion oscillates unceasingly and slips to the right and to the left without a clear decision becoming possible. Someone might tell me that these discussions don't take place so as to come to a decision inasmuch as they concern opinion. I would respond that it does not interest me then that the discussion between intellectuals, the famous "debate," is a sterile and vain operation – Pascal said uncertain – an impossible decision, something on the order of an aporia that brings us back to a certain sophistry, about which I spoke at the beginning of our conversation.

PP: *Even so, you admit that there may be local debates. Debates between experts, for example: regulating scallop fishing, is that not a debate for you? So in what situations can we talk about impossible debate?*

FL: The example that you are talking about is not one between intellectuals, and so only the scallops, who deserve better, would be able to make the decision . . . More seriously, the more that debate steps outside of restrictive scientific parameters, the more it becomes undecidable: the same kind of undecidable debate as the debate between philosophers. One philosopher always appears to get the upper hand over another, but all of that is purely local and does not imply a decision into the truth. The intellectuals are each other's hostages and even form a double hostage system. Even in Levinas, of course, I am a hostage to the Other, but it wouldn't take much for the Other to be my hostage and the object of my persecution. In any case, at the level of "horizontal" discussion, the intellectuals are reciprocally prisoners to their own argumentation. Deleuze was right to say that debates are useless, except when they are used by philosophy itself which wins hands down, triumphing over the combatants. The philosophers exaggerate in order to make this system work without asking themselves about the mode in which it functions and about the limits of dialog, exchange, and all their derived concepts.

PP: *How can the Gordian knot be cut? How can a decision be made if reference to empirical facts is never sufficient to determine a decision?*

FL: The invocation of facts of the scientific kind or of historical and political givens does not suffice, indeed, to necessitate a decision. So, between these reciprocal hostages who are intellectuals in a debate, it is necessary to introduce another term which, not being empirically or ideally given, will loosen the ring that holds them in an iron grip. The only term that can free them is the Name-of-Man and so the Name-of-the-Victim. She alone determines the intellectuals in their relationship, a relationship that is no longer one of reciprocal ascendancy but of a common side-by-side struggle. Of course, I understand that this description is a little radical and abstract because in every intellectual discussion someone invokes either political facts or ideological motivations. But the problem is not one of disengaging absolutely from the intellectuals, but of disengaging them from their reciprocal conflicts by engaging them with the victims. They can engage in debate on the basis of being first engaged in comparison with victims.

Reality is in a state of permanent auto-dissolution. All of its criteria are themselves grounded or immerse themselves in the vast immanence of the World and in the permanent exchange of arguments. All the great attributes – history, language, sex, power, politics, and even reason – lose their consistency and enter into the order of the simulacrum. The simulacrum is not complete, meaning that we are not within Deleuze's philosophy here. Thanks to Nietzsche and Spinoza, Deleuze pushed this state of the World's auto-dissolution and auto-affirmation to its limit. As I have previously said, for the victims who are transformed into persecutors and vice versa, this is a principle which allows a certain sense, a local sense at least, to be given to those phenomena of indecision or the inhibition of decision. The inhibition of decision remains a big problem. We inhibit decision by multiplying decisions. The presupposed of the intellectual, those who have a "condition," is not the reciprocal exchange of arguments which dissolves every presupposed. He needs an irreducible presupposed, the Name-of-the-Victim, which comes to prepare him so as to intervene otherwise, that is what gets him into a position of struggle or, better still, into the spirit of struggle. I speak of a spirit of struggle like we speak of a spirit of music, of poetry . . . I prefer to speak of the spirit of struggle rather than of struggle, because struggle assumes that we are already engaged in combat. Whereas the spirit of struggle prepares for it, it is the condition for combat, this condition being here negative or non-sufficient.

This is it, the Name-of-the-Victim is a non-sufficient conditioning [*mise-en-condition*] for the intellectual subject and for his discourse.

PP: *So you are taking a completely inverted position in relation to Homeric courage. Would the true courage be to retreat from the victims?*

FL: No, the true courage is not to retreat from the victims because it is the Victim who causes this "retreat," if need be. But this retreat is not a flight. On the contrary, it is what happens to put the intellectual in a position to use the weapons of politics, history, and philosophy. Later on, I will talk about how this apparent retreat is instead a dimension of radical arrival affecting the intellectual subject, something like a future that the Victim-in-person brings with her to the intellectual. If the intellectual subject is immediately engaged in conflict, as we have seen with our intellectuals who rush to their weapons, a little worn-out in their hands, then he is immediately taken up into a relationship of reciprocity, semblance, from hostage to hostage, so much so that the winner is neither this hostage nor that one, but philosophy, master of the double bind and the Gordian knot. They are happy with ruling [*faire marcher*] over history, even when they critique it. I agree with Badiou when he said that our current intellectuals have remained too Kantian, too concerned with critique, but I would not go as far as saying, as he does, that we must immediately take the courageous stance and one of actual resistance. That seems to me another philosophical solution, anti-Kantian but much too . . . spontaneous.

PP: *But there are moments when the historical situation allows for nothing else but to begin actual resistance. I am picking up on the example of Cavaillès again.*

FL: I do not mean to say that the intellectual needs a moment of reflection in order to understand something "is at stake" and that he has to put off the moment. On the contrary, that would be fatal for him. But if he refers to the Victim, there is a moment which is not awaiting or suspending struggle, but refusing what Descartes called haste. For all that, it holds struggle back. This is what I call *a priori defense*, in order to differentiate it from auto-defense or the style of auto-security. He practices neither holding back nor hastening. He practices what I will call the radical future. He takes the only distance that does not move him away from struggle but also does not push him into struggle, rather he takes the distance through which *he comes there or is called to struggle without means*. To go and meet conflict is quite a different thing from falling into combat. This arrival allows him to grab a hold of the means of struggle provided by the context and transform them according to the concrete Victim, who is inside the regime of the World or history. The determined intellectual does not enter into struggle without being in a state that destabilizes *a priori* the humanitarian concern of the dominant intellectual.

So a weapon must not be utilized by another weapon or by a hand that would itself become a weapon. A weapon is at least double-sided or -edged, phenomenologically so. The pragmatic, here, is not simply a question of the usage of the means provided. It concerns a usage which transforms the weapons in their very conscription or in making them one-sided or *single-edged* [*uni-tranchant*]. As the Victim-in-person is unrepresentable, she suspends the simple reaction to representation and forces the reaction. Are you going to ask me what she forces it into? Into the transformation that I am going to implement here in practice, that of the cutting edge in the single-edged blade, and that is an intellectual intervention. I am saying no more than that.

PP: *We could summarize things in the following way: the determined intellectual must get himself into a state of the spirit of struggle so as to not participate in the domination and vanity of certain debates and, it should be said, in debate in general. This is a necessary condition, but is it a sufficient condition?*

FL: Of course not. In this disjunction between necessity and sufficiency, there is an abyss for philosophy because philosophy has a tendency to hold them simultaneously: that which is necessary is in general sufficient. According to an expression of the Heideggerian kind, I can say that the intellectual is thrown into the victims, but that does not mean that he is *in the midst* of victims. And in fact, even though he is not in the midst of them, he can struggle *for* them, which is not a way out. But, thrown into the victims, he no longer has a choice. He takes them as they present themselves, all the while knowing that they are local victims and that there are no paradigmatic conflicts, no absolutely crucial debates, none more fundamental or more exemplary than others.

PP: *What does he transform, this determined intellectual? Is it not reality? We cannot say that he created an event for thought any more. What is the notion that would correspond to this kind of use of weapons?*

FL: The Victim of some abuse or some persecution is in reality a victim twice. There is not only the status of fact, there is also the interpretation of this status. A spontaneous interpretation for the Victim herself because she cannot psychologically interpret her being-persecuted as being sufficient, being amidst the cruelty or the misfortune. The state of persecution creates in the Victim a kind of faith or belief in her being-persecuted. So an act of persecution assumes itself to have a certain legitimacy. The protests of the Victim, from this point of view and if they exist, are not always very clear because they are very close to a demand for vengeance or reparation and that reparation reproduces an entire state of things which is precisely what is in question here. Even crying out "mercy!," a prayer, even though that would be the least she could ask, can sometimes be understood as a weapon, the request recognized by the executioner and received by the Victim as a gift or a "grace." It is this (double) belief and this representation which is able to be transformed with the victims.

PP: *Mandela and Tutu did not demand vengeance. They did not, for that matter, declare general amnesty, but amnesty case by case.*

FL: Do you believe that a case-by-case basis, the singularity rather than the generality, is the condition by which justice will finally be found? This is contemporary philosophy, which is full of meaning within history, but not full of meaning for the plane which determines it.

PP: *But it is no longer a question anymore of being on some philosophical terrain. Not throwing oneself into conflict but going ahead of the conflict, putting oneself in the service of the victim, does that mean that it is necessary to determine the terms of conflict so that reality is transformed instead of repeated?*

FL: Intellectuals and philosophers have always examined the problems from the past and the *de facto* situation by assuming the problems to be determinate. In this framework, the idea of the Victim-in-person is unthinkable. She introduces a backwards logic [*logique à rebours*] which, on the contrary, consists of examining the conflicts and transforming the terms for the future, in the Name-of-Man. What I call the future is effectively the same thing that I call the spirit of struggle and holds to human identity.

PP: *But if there is a victim it is because there is a conflict.*

FL: Yes, conflict always precedes, but the Victim-in-person does not react to conflict, she does not insert herself into the same temporality as that of the philosophers, where the past engenders the past. We must ask that just once the event produce itself from the future. The Victim-in-person is not representable, she is an empty function as regards temporal or other representations, but she does make the determined intellectual act. The dominant intellectual rushes into the idea that he forges himself out of conflict, he battles indefinitely within the void of appearances so that the determined intellectual acts through this void that he is and takes as presupposed. This is a quasi-Eastern formula . . .

PP: *But when the philosopher intervenes as an intellectual, he does so precisely in the name of a temporality which is not the market temporality of the general equivalent. Isn't philosophy what also subtracts itself from the World and claims to create those conditions for thought that are different from those conditions for the continuous flow of the media and commodities?*

FL: The philosopher effectively eludes the World but this is always so that he can return to it. This round-trip is his proper gesture, and so it is also that of the dominant intellectual. However, what I call the Victim-in-person does not elude [*se soustrait*] history, she is already excluded [*soustraite*] there. So she goes out to history or to the World. I have always said, as when I wrote the book on non-Marxism, that I am not repeating Marxism, but that I would go to Marxism. It is a going out without a return, there was no going out before the return nor a return after the going out. There is a single vector, a single movement, I call it unilateral.

PP: *You repress something of philosophy in this simple going out.*

FL: In reality this expression of a single going out or a single coming is still a little too simple. On the whole, it is a going out from the Victim-in-person for history, meaning towards the represented victims. But in reality there is a complex phase, such that intellectual goes out to history and to the victims but as already known *a priori* by the future or by the Victim-in-person. In fact, there is a single genuine movement, that of the intellectual, but the Victim-in-person is not in motion, the radical future is a-temporal.

PP: *When we say "give yourself to the Victim-in-person" as presupposed, what is the exact function of "giving oneself?" Insofar as it does not restore a dialectical gesture and insofar as the same term of going out or coming designates a movement of thought, what is it about this "giving oneself" that can produce effects upon the World? Is it because even if this does not transform the concrete World, it does transform the philosophical materials that allow us usage of the World?*

FL: Transforming the World by remaining in it is not a function the determined intellectual has. His function consists in making a new sphere of existence – his own – emerge: I call this sphere the subject. The determined intellectual is not a subject x or y who would fulfil this exterior function. But it is x or y who becomes a subject as a determined intellectual. The entire problem is one of constituting the sphere of intellectual existence along with that of the history-world: – a sphere which gets into trouble with history and politics since it constantly nourishes itself with the World but whose principle is not within the World. This is what I call, along with other names, the city of heretics.

Regarding the first aspect of your question, indeed, the expression "give yourself to the Victim-in-person" can be very dangerous because it looks like it posits an act of givenness. In other words, the being of the Victim would resolve itself within an intellectual act of positioning. That would be idealist. It is not that, of course. The position of the Victim-in-person is an intellectual act, of language and of thinking together, but such that this position is not an auto-position, but an act already determined in-the-last-instance, a position that is non-positional (of) itself. So, in reality, we do not give ourselves to the Victim, she is given, even if she appears posited within the order of thought-language. This position is an intellectual act which does not go on to exhaust its being real, which is foreclosed there. This idea of a real presupposed of thought is an absolutely anti-idealist notion and I would also say anti-materialist, but this is difficult to handle if one isn't used to doing philosophy.

# The Practice of the Determined Intellectual

PP: *Before we get into the city of heretics and establish still more exactly, once and for all, what non-philosophy can do [les pouvoirs de la non-philosophie], can you specify again the status of the determined intellectual in relation to the forest of interpretations that you have spoken about. What is his role?*

FL: The non-humanitarian intellectual works under the Name-of-Man. This is the general formula for his purpose [*objet*]: combat the spontaneous belief that wants a complete crime-form to exist. Crime would at once: (1) fill up every intimate space there is for humans or alienate them as Men; (2) be fought against under this form in an effective, direct, and local way. This belief is, of course, contradictory and philosophically or dialectically resolves itself. The determined intellectual does not reverse this belief, he inverts it: (1) Man-in-person is not affected by crime, it is the subject alone who is affected by crime and who engages in a struggle for liberation; (2) in practice, the determined intellectual refuses and invalidates the complete crime-form that puts forward the dominant intellectual as valid. If I were a Hegelian, I would say that the determined intellectual is the consciousness of the engaged intellectual. But the determined intellectual is precisely also engaged but is engaged otherwise, not according to the reign of the consciousness of oneself and absolute knowledge, but that of the Victim-in-person.

By crime-form, I do not mean the famous "modus operandi" which characterizes those individuals, states, or ethnic groups that are identified as criminal. These modi operandi are multiple. In the immediate past there was the Nazi-exterminator style, the Stalinist-judicial style, there is the democratico-terrorist style of the American way, the ethno-purifiers, etc. – history has invented a great many (the inquisitorial style, for example, and the style of harassment) by adding the complement of the police style to all of them: "police operations," torture and the deprivation of rights, finally the various forms of confinement and concentration. The crime-form, on the contrary, is one of history's universal forms or attributes, that can only allow the Victim-in-person to be apperceived. Of course, we have to demonstrate this crime-form of history, which is actual, in order to make out the multitude of victims, who have already been consumed or who are still virtual, those who make up the ground of history.

PP: *But then isn't there an inevitability to history?*

FL: I am not expressing an opinion about inevitability or fate. History is not necessary without being contingent, and without being necessary a second time in the higher and comprehensive [*globale*] way. The determined intellectual must work up a general hypothesis about the meaning of history, regarding our problem, of course, which states that hypothesis. This general hypothesis, as we have said of victimization, is that every victim can in turn become a persecutor. Difficult to admit, but insofar as history is supposed to form a self-including and thus immanent system, we cannot conceive victimization except in this way and so we submit to it, except for those little casuistry exceptions carried out case-by-case according to incomplete doctrines or, so to speak, "by request." A complementary hypothesis is imposed upon us which claims that the engaged intellectual has his way of participating in crime. Participating in its prevention and its redress, he allows it to survive in the same regime. If there is some inevitability, then what subjects the dominant intellectual to that structure is that inevitability.

PP: *You say that we cannot redeem crime. But can we prevent it?*

FL: The struggle not against crime – because crime is necessarily at least half the story – but against the dominant faith in crime can happen without the religious fantasy of redemption. As for preventing it, we can only prevent it from inside the cycle of vengeance, or more generally from inside history. History is only a set of operations that prepare for crime, preventing it and redeeming it, operations that are nearly simultaneous over the long term, – this is what makes man a being that can be victimized.

---

PP: *At the start of the conversation, you said that there were wars which had been necessary. So you have a double postulate.*

FL: In fact, there is a unilateral duality of postulates, or rather of heterogeneous givens. There is not a unique or double postulation because that is what philosophy calls itself, but this is the unilateral side of the postulation entirely. Regarding history, it is necessary by definition to intervene in it, maybe sometimes through a war but not necessarily preventative wars, because that is an extremely dangerous concept, but through precautions taken in order to limit, if not prevent, crime. Still, in general, it is very difficult to prevent crime, which has something so conjectural, so accidental, about it that, in one sense, it is never predictable. But what happens in history does not interest me here, except insofar as I can make out of it an occasion or material. I am indicating that the *a priori* defense of the Victim, by which I mean the determined intellectual, is nearly the exact opposite of preventative war, the abuse of power above all others, the law of terror by the strong.

PP: *Is the determined intellectual induced to work the materials of the dominant intellectual?*

FL: Of course. He himself has no fundamental kind of material, as philosophy does, and nothing like the regional kind of material, as the sciences do. His only specific object is the dominant intellectual's (double) belief in all-history, in all-politics. This specific object, the World, is carried, transported, by historical circumstances and situations.

PP: *Isn't this an ethical practice? For example, in* Lacan's Ethics of Psychoanalysis, *in the seminar on the good where he takes goods as an image of the good, he speaks of praxis in order to better show that there is no regulative ideal of the good but simply a practice of useful goods.*

FL: This is not particularly an ethical practice. The term "practice" as I use it has a much more general sense. In the past I have sometimes insisted on the theoretical aspect of non-philosophy. It is effectively a theory, but it is a practice of theory. It is a practice because there is a radical transformation imposed by the presupposed on all the procedures that have been historically elaborated around crime. The principle of this unilateral transformation or practice is the following. The Victim-in-person is herself indifferent to every action or operation of history – this is a first name. But as for what language is used, what means of thought called for, all of that comes from history and is used first by the dominant intellectual. The determined intellectual is also obliged to make some use of it, because he only has these means at his disposal. We have to understand that the Victim-in-person, because she is foreign to history, comes out of an extreme poverty: she has nothing for herself. The determined intellectual takes everything from elsewhere but he makes another usage of it. This other usage is not a simple pragmatic because these means taken from history are not simply related, as they are, to a human subject who becomes the Victim as a generality. They are only related to the Victim-in-person who transformed them through unilaterality and her strange incomplete duality. The Victim-in-person is a blank screen and everything that comes from history and that is projected on that screen has no surety upon the screen itself. It is that "blank" screen which makes the victims appear for history, not under another representation or image, but as a phenomenon. By image, we mean a simple reproduction, a double of the thing assumed to exist by itself. By phenomenon, we mean the simple being-given or lived (of) identity, this identity where the thing assumed to be in-itself and its representation are fused together but transformed.

PP: *Since the determined intellectual notices that history is spinning and that the dominant intellectuals are only marking time [*surplace*], what does the determined intellectual do to avoid merely marking time like this?*

FL: He doesn't move [*se déplace*], but from the outset emplaces all displacements. We distinguish between the signifying and Lacanian place, the Marxist and materialist displacements, the dominant stand-still [*surplace*] or Nietzschean overview [*survol*], the emplace that Man-in-person produces for philosophy or the World, and finally the without-place of the Real or utopia of Man. For now, these are the same thing, this isn't a time to wait, to see what happens, or to delay, but now as a future coming to the present, to time itself, but never within time – the future does not fall into the present. Man-in-person is a future-without-time. There is a dimension of exteriority due to the immanence of being human which affects the whole of history. In fact, the determined intellectual gives the dominant intellectual his presupposed. He transforms the action in a practice that has a presupposed, and the great presupposed is Man-in-Man and what I call his messianity.

PP: *Can we ask the question of atheism here? Religions are from now on more than ever the object of a particular treatment on the part of dominant intellectuals. The idea is that the function of religion comes back to haunt the symbolic universe of humans. It is sort of, for better and for worse, the eternal symbol that we just have to hold on to. What is the function for you of atheism – is it a function?*

FL: It is not exactly a function but a posture. The kind of atheism that I call radical, and not absolute, does not deny the religions or the religious function. I accept that there has been a religious culture, indeed a religious belief. *Future Christ* also confirms it in a certain way. It concerns the Messiah who is every man. But just as I do not leave philosophy to its own authority, so I do not leave theology or religious beliefs to their own authorities. Nevertheless, this is exactly what the dominant intellectuals do when they claim to return to religion. I am not returning to religion, the Future Christ does not announce a conversion but an inversion of history. I come to religion as I come to philosophy, for something else, and I come there for the first and so the last time. Absolute atheism only leads to a new religion. We are not going to simply return to Malraux's formula which says that the century to come, our own, will be religious. What can be humanly done with religion, that is the true question. The concern here is not with becoming believers again, because in general we are too faithful even when we do not believe ourselves to be so. It also is not about leaning against belief again in order to return to the thesis, so obvious nevertheless, of a war of religion.

PP: *How do you see your relation to the question of the theologico-political? Since you are interested in Marxism, is the theologico-political more than just an epistemological obstacle?*

FL: Of course. This is the problem of global resistance of what I call philosophy or the resistance of the history-world. Certainly we have to slip through the net of resistance, into its cracks, its faults, but we also must rightly and systematically put forward the right of this resistance. I owe this provocation to some adversaries I can't be reconciled with, and it is very good this way. Because it is a resistance of philosophy created by non-philosophy, like the analytic act creates or activates some resistance in the analysand. The institutionalization of psychoanalysis has been slow and has not happened without causing damage, and if there is to be an institutionalization for non-philosophy it will be slow and will not happen without causing damage either. We have already seen the first effects.

PP: *Let's continue the description of the determined intellectual's general traits.*

FL: There are several characteristics that you must have in mind for what follows. On the one hand, the Victim-in-person is a negative condition – that is, not a positive condition which the determined intellectual would deduce from himself. Secondly, within the limits of this negative condition, the determined intellectual is constrained from going somewhere else to draw the means of his own practice, but instead draws them from the only reservoir possible, that of history. Thirdly, the determined intellectual has a practice rather than an action. Usually we understand a practice as an action or an activity, but the action immediately interlocks with a reaction. The action can be active as Nietzsche said but it is also fundamentally reactionary, so also "vengeful." That is to say that practice cannot confine itself to the circle of action and reaction, it transforms the given and *de jure* inert material. Even if the material was not inert to start off with, it has been made inert in the sense that it has been relived of history's sufficiency. Practice is therefore immanent in its way, because there is no practice which is purely exterior. Its immanent principle is that it forms itself in-the-last-humaneity. Action is always taken in the labyrinth of vengeance, whereas practice transforms the labyrinth without entering it. Fourthly, these means taken from within history are deprived of their auto-reflection or their auto-determination, of their absolute sufficiency, and are liberated from the cycle of vengeance by the style of unilaterality.

PP: *How are action and practice distinguished, since you are making that distinction?*

FL: Action is a hugely idealist concept, which prevents its auto-legitimization. Practice is not acting in the idealist sense of the word, except if it is expressly recuperated by the great idealist philosophies of Kant and, in particular, Fichte, and Hegel secondarily. Action obeys the more or less ideal norms, but it also produces its own norms;

whereas practice always has a presupposed that limits the pretension to self-organization or self-legislation. Practice has norms that constitute it as a practice but which it cannot itself unceasingly remodel or reinvent within an interminable project. It transforms the materials, whatever these materials may be, even intellectual materials, but practice does not recreate them in its own image. Moreover, an "active" intellectual has a single language and single action at his disposal. There is an appearance of performativity in his work in the sense of an appearance of very strict communication between what he says and what he does. That he protests in a newspaper or signs a petition is enough to believe that this effect, which is grounded in the last resort on his belief in history and philosophy rather than in victims, presses down on history itself and by implication his identity. This is spontaneous belief, a true "natural attitude" which thinks that the real content of action is acquired and exhausted by this faith, whereas the determined intellectual is performative in-the-last-instance alone, in the name of the Victim. He is not performative except in what he does, and he knows it. Finally, action reproduces images or doubles of itself, it produces representation, while practice destroys representations. It uses, at a pinch, the presentation of a phenomenon without reproducing doublets. Practice does not mark time [*surplace*].

PP: *What would be the presupposed of Art or Science?*

FL: Let us assume that these would be, in my language, two practices. I define a practice, in order to distinguish it from philosophy, by a double presupposed: one of the language or "metalanguage" necessary in order to constitute it, the other of reality or the real object in order to give it its consistency.

PP: *You say that philosophy is always the re-appropriation of some essence, but philosophy also offers the possibility of not shrinking away from a point of indistinction or indiscernability. There is this idea of not giving in to what approaches. This is therefore the re-appropriation of a void that, by definition, is not given as an essence. You are neither in the midst of the re-appropriation of some essence nor the re-appropriation of some unnamable point.*

FL: Man-in-person is neither namable nor unnamable. Precisely it is this way of thinking, metaphysically and mystically, that has to change – these are not the terms. The Victim-in-person is what determines a subject for the complex relation of the nameable and the unnamable. Most of the time what we call a void is only a stasis within a movement of thought even if we posit it as absolute. Man-in-person is not an absolute void nor a point of indecision, he is a radical void of determination and I distinguish very carefully between radical and absolute. Because radical here means that there is nothing at all to empirical determinations, but that is only a consequence. It is a void whose nature is to be through immanence. It is a void-in-void. So, of course, if we try to represent this void, we won't get there and we will protest at the word-play . . . How can we not give philosophers a referral for the couch?

PP: *But he escapes the truth, then?*

FL: He escapes the truth. Hence the idea that Man-in-person is not the object of truth, he is the true-without-truth. The true does not proceed from truth, it has primacy over the truth. We can call it the true or the non-true, in fact it does not matter, because it is what will determine in-the-last-instance the relations which form the truth. But Man-in-person is foreclosed to truth.

PP: *Because he is foreclosed to every logic of being?*

FL: Exactly, to every logic. I have to recognize that this will offend common sense and so the understanding such as it has been formed by the corpus of philosophies. In reality, this thought is much less irrational than we would be able to imagine. I do not mean that it is rational but only to underline the fact that practices, as much scientific practice as artistic or religious practice, have a certain affinity with non-philosophy. Practices have their presupposeds, unlike philosophy which only has presuppositions – presupposeds that they cannot then reappropriate like we reappropriate presuppositions. They are definitive, they are not only first, they have primacy over these activities themselves. The presupposed of non-philosophy is the Name-of-Man which cannot be reappropriated, but it is Man-in-Man who appropriates the World. So, we are clearly doomed [*voués*] in history, but we are not necessarily thrown *into* history. We are even *for* history in the sense that we work for its radical critique and its transformation.

PP: *Your Man-in-person then appropriates history without joining in with the desire to protect himself from*

*history, isolating himself in it ... For example when
Baudrillard talks about radical thought, he talks about
a thought which would play out history and globalization in a completely different way as being capable of
no longer joining in with the logic of history's power.
Can we not avoid evoking this idea of protection that
is being given to us here in order to better go to history,
as you say?*

FL: I am not cutting myself off in the sense that there
are no previous operations for getting outside of history. I am not cutting myself off because I am isolated,
and I doubt that philosophers and intellectuals can
understand that. More exactly, Man – I am not saying
the subject – is a solitude that has not extracted itself
out of history but that is *for* history. It is in going there
that one becomes a subject. Man is an abstract solicited
by history, so one takes the posture of the subject-
existing-Intellectual or determined intellectual. We can
always say that putting forth such an axiom is a way of
fleeing. From the point of view of philosophy, you can
say anything, philosophy doesn't mind. On that point
I have nothing to say in response, certainly not. My
problem is that of creating effects within the theory of
history, within the theory of justice. That these effects
are refused in the name of urgency, the empirical practice of the intellectuals, I understand that entirely. But I
am not going to respond to that argument because it is a
vicious argument which auto-legitimates itself, it strictly
proves nothing, except its own existence, as always a
little stupid. To shout about [*Clamer*] its existence does
not prove its reality. There, my argument is Kantian,
but even so it is solid enough. What is actually useful

when it proclaims its usefulness is this clamour, look at the *cogito*.

PP: *What I simply wanted to say was that Man-in-person cannot not come into history.*

FL: Non-Philosophy justifies the constraint, the necessity of our contingent relation to the World. Non-Philosophy, in a general way, is what we could call a theory of Everything [*théorie du Tout*]. How is a theory of Everything possible? A theory of Everything must necessarily borrow its theoretical means from the Whole [*Tout*] itself. But a philosophy cannot be a theory of Everything since the means that it uses will be taken from the Whole and remain presuppositions without being presupposed. It will not be the theory of its own means. Only non-philosophy resolves this problem because it is capable of borrowing its means from the Whole, history, politics, philosophy, all while forming the theory of borrowing and usage of these means. In doing this it is no longer quite a simple theory, it is a practice of theory. A non-philosopher can only look for a theory of Everything, of the pretension of philosophy to totalize. We are condemned to philosophy just as we are to history, condemned to confront the global crime-form. The non-philosopher is who deals with this project of totalizing by trying to create its theory without joining the game of totalization, but by using it.

PP: *What do you mean by a mode of intervention that would not fall prey to philosophical urgency? And can you first clarify what you are calling philosophical urgency?*

FL: Urgency is always the actuality of urgency. Urgency is actual and strains actuality so that the intellectual is brought to work just in the nick of time. We have already said that philosophy is a system of thought preceding in advance and also through delay. In advance because it projects possible solutions before having even really lived the situations. But this permanent anticipation is at the same time a permanent delay on the event. Philosophy, wedged between this anticipation and this delay, is then in an imminent position and sometimes an impotent position with the feeling of having arrived too late. Urgency is a temporality that is held back, compressed, brought up too short and always in the process of an auto-overcoming. The feeling of catastrophe that the intellectuals often have has something to do with millenarism, but this is millenarism over a short distance, a brief messianism. The absence or the shadow of that final, great nuclear catastrophe causes this time of action to break up into a multiplicity of imminent catastrophes, flashes, and emergencies. These intellectuals are not putting forth the hypothesis that we have not seen anything yet of what we are going to see, or rather anything of what we should have "to see" – this is the worst actuality [*l'actualité du pire*], a hypothesis that immanent messianity requires. The hypothesis of a menacing universal chaos only sustains philosophy and its dominant master, Reason. The hypothesis of the worst actuality is the equivalent for history, but it would have to allow thought to "invert" the intellectual ideal.

PP: *Insofar as current events determine a good deal of our representations and insofar as the circle of historical reason continues to turn, the drama of current events is being subjected to the imperative for news and to the imperative for results. But is it that this subjection, this compressed temporality as you said, holds the media within the same form as the production [mise en scène] of reality, or even that it holds the philosophy of history in this way? Where is it that they both meet?*

FL: It is not a question of disengaging from current events. We are condemned to them like the rest. The concern is with "making do" and with "doing otherwise." How to transform current events while working with them is the problem for non-philosophy. How to make do without reproducing what is empirically given in its own explanation. We are in the world of reflection, of permanent simulacra, of the redundancy of information, which ends in a kind of dissolution of history and time in their implosion and their auto-simulation. So-called "real time" is in reality always lagging on itself because the event has always already taken place and will already be reproduced with some family resemblance just as we receive the image of it. But the future is the room for maneuvering around the present and which comes ahead of the present. It does not fully leave the present so as to be projected into a to-come [*avenir*]. It comes as an ultimatum for the present. This future [*futur*] that constantly arrives, and that we have a tendency to erase, to forget in favor of the present's heaviness, indeed of the heaviness of the past, this future unceasingly emerges ahead of us . . .

PP: *This ultimatum to the present is a way of saying that man is not a being in the world.*

---

FL: Exactly. The future does not come out of some temporal transcendence, it comes from the depths of human immanence. It comes from Man-in-Man to the subject. It is from the ground of immanence that the future emerges and not from the heights of transcendence. Of course, everything presses on us to act, to short-circuit reflection in order to act and to turn the reflection into an action. One could think that the intellectual I am describing takes his time. But that is not altogether the case here, because he is not situated within a unitary temporality. He takes time backwards and gives it.

PP: *And what becomes then of* kairos? *The opportune moment, the opportune decision? As philosophies of action are linked to philosophies of the subject, can there be an order of action here that will not be a decision of the subject?*

FL: The term "action," as I have already told you, bothers me because of its idealist character which assumes a space of simultaneity, indeed of unity, between action and the event itself. And so of a break between an action and a reaction, because, if things are really simultaneous, there is inevitably a reaction which follows on from the action. I prefer the term "practice." Practice never truly has the totality of its conditions in itself. Man determines practice, meaning that if there is a decision it will have its identity at that time, an identity that we can call non-decisional (of) itself. This is not a decision that grounds itself upon itself like the decision for action. If we turn the multiplicity of practices, with their heterogeneous characteristics, their own languages, and their own objects, if we turn that multiplicity towards the general idea of a praxis, we risk drowning all this diversity in a philosophy of action. Action is a thought with presuppositions, it has presupposeds that action itself claims to posit and that it recovers. But the presupposeds are irreducible or untransformable through practice itself, which must let itself be determined by them. The dominant intellectual has an action that comes with all the reflections, idealizations, and redoublings which are linked to belief in the all-powerfulness of action, while the non-humanitarian intellectual simply has a more modest practice which does not have the ambition to totalize itself.

PP: *How do you define* kairos?

FL: Philosophical *kairos* is the instant of the simultaneity of contraries, so therefore of being and becoming. It is the moment of absolute coincidence between them. It is a blessed, happy moment, as Deleuze said. But here is the thing, there is no longer any *kairos* under this form for the Victim/intellectual couple. What we can recover from *kairos* is that the non-humanitarian intellectual is turned according-to-the-future towards a represented victim, whom he does not choose since the Victim is within the panorama of representation. But he turns himself as though towards the Victim, whom he pulls out of the self-sufficiency of her representation. This is what gives him his temporal identity or his present, which makes him drop into the "occasion." This is what I call the World or history in the state of an occasion. The occasion is the moment when the future of the Victim-in-person sends the intellectual to a victim, and this sending off makes the Victim more than a singularity, an identity.

PP: *We are close to the* factum?

FL: Yes and no. Because the future is also what is sent ahead of the subject. This is not what is before us, because it comes from nowhere, but it comes ahead of . . . I am close enough here to certain themes of Levinas, except that this is not an Other, it is Man-in-person who manifests and who opens the philosophical closure of history through a radical immanence, not by way of some transcendence.

PP: *This future that comes from elsewhere is moreover a breaking out of the time of philosophy.*

FL: From nowhere, rather than from elsewhere – that would be to redouble it. The subject only escapes the auto-alienated times of philosophy because he is snatched or determined by a future that comes towards him, in front of historical time. Man-in-person is not an escape, is not a flight. On the other hand, the Intellectual-subject is at the same time thrown into history and separated, forced to withdraw, to dis-alienate himself from history by way of his always future subject position. The non-humanitarian intellectual is not necessarily someone who would refuse to go to demonstrations, someone who would refuse to sign petitions. He looks for another usage. He can absolutely participate in these things, but he will not limit his own action to the belief that sustains them.

# Criminal History and the Demand for Justice

PP: *Jankelevitch said that heroes do not hold a conference on heroism. The critical intellectual sees crime. He denounces it, but he's an addict now. Evil is, for him, an encounter that he cannot resolve himself to call off. So can't consciousness of crime clear our names before the requirement of justice? How do you resolve this aporia?*

FL: A society conscious of crime, and so criminal twice over (and this is what we are), demands a new critique of intellectual reason. It is a criminal society also because in every respect the criminal is still privileged in relation to the victim. There has always been, in the couple that forms the criminal and his victim, an ontological primacy of the first, a primacy of reality, of dignity, and of *logos* – history as reason and propaganda of the victors, victory as the sufficient reason of history. But new circumstances have brought forth an injustice more profound than that of a judgment that victims would suffer under, something like a nonjudgment, an absence of judgment for victims who are always "spectators" (I am thinking of the heretics, the remembrance of whom is regularly scoffed at). It makes one suspect that the judgment concerning criminals takes place between them and the third instance of Justice, between declared powers in a demonstrative competition. It took the Jewish people, this is an example of that decision, to rebel themselves against this forgetting of victims for a new situation to emerge and to compel everyone to think otherwise. This is not without danger, of course, because after all it is not certain that justice for the victims consists in demanding judgment, memory, and reparation; it is not certain that victims are satisfied with being the instigators of a simple judgment concerning their executioners.

PP: *What place do you give to "the example," as you said, of the Shoah?*

FL: Victims are never examples (a revisionist concept) but the revolt of the Jewish people is "exemplary." The problem lies here. Is there perhaps a Jewish excess of victims since the Victim "asks for justice" in a hyperbolic way? An excess on top of justice and also on top of the Victim. The Jewish people can put themselves in the position of "plaintiffs associated with the prosecutor" [*parties civiles*], but cannot specify the judgment, even if it is one of "memory," without the threat of taking up an ambiguous place. To "demand" or "ask for" justice, that's progress in the theory of victims, but it is also a problematic position, a position of reclaiming [*revendication*] which forms a circle or system with violence and prolongs this makeshift solution, calling itself "rendering-Justice-with-a-capital-J." The rendering of justice, its givenness, quickly becomes a sufficient justice. Concerning the Shoah, I have made myself clear about it in *Future Christ*.

PP: *So are there really victims, or are they not victims if they come back badly into the usual apparatus, the triad of criminal, victim, and judge (as representing the legislator)?*

FL: To demand justice as a right marked by its rarity, this inserts the Victim as a piece into a system of which the act of rendering justice will be the synthesis. How are a synthetic judgment (between the parties) and an *a priori* judgment (justice as transcendental principle) possible? It concerns breaking precisely with this kind of solution. But "to demand" is also to postulate. The Victim postulates it, not consequently as a desired or required thing, not even asking for it as a hypothesis for some future deduction of its right. Postulating justice as necessary without representing it within the World or within history, forcing it without asking for it is possible if its postulation coincides with the being-given of the Victim-in-person. Justice as justification of a subject has as a final cause the Victim and is not only this assemblage of institutions that produces nothing whatsoever that resembles such a subject. The justice-world is a synthesis based upon a demand or a desire, *the-Victim-who-demands-justice.* We can imagine instead a *victim-who-determines-the-demand-for-justice-without-relying-on-the-sufficiency-of-the-demand.* The Victim-in-person is one postulated without an act of postulation, an anhypothetical hypothesis, and this without philosophical blending. The Victim does not project an ideal justice within transcendence, except if she goes along with vengeance. To determine the demand for justice is of course not sufficient in order to effectively produce it: the Victim is insufficient there. This is instead *giving-in-Man justice as demanded*, which is the exact definition of the anaxiomatic axiom, whereby the real instance of the Victim immediately assumes this demand for justice formulated by the intellectual.

PP: *There is nevertheless an acting for justice when it concerns victims – does it have a certain effectiveness? I have made an allusion to it with the South African "truth and reconciliation" commission.*

FL: Victims can win victories in the long term, but that will not go beyond the judgment and punishment concerning the criminal in the best of cases. That criminals may finally be judged is the victims' problematic victory, always woven somewhat into a differed and regulated vengeance, with reparations. But in most historical cases, there is no "reparation." However, what is important does not lie here. The Victim is in the state of solitary multiplicity, already lost and uninteresting as much as the criminal is interesting. There is a science of criminals, there is no such science of the victim, just psychological treatment, and maybe she is fortunate this way; the sign that the Victim is of a different nature from the criminal is that she is unthinkable. Those philosophers who gladly speak with some contempt for the "rhetoric of victimhood" are hardly moved by the Victim. In the terms of the greatest philosopher of history, Hegel, we could say that the criminal shows up on the scene of history (*Schauplatz*) or remains within his enclosure, while the Victim falls outside of the historical scene and returns to the earth which lacks spirit, and which is not always ours, to the ashes where all is black and grey, without any possible distinction or ideality. Of course since a victim like the Jewish people began to refuse this customary forgetting, which for a long time they themselves had tolerated, philosophy no longer knows "where to turn" and does not understand that there is no longer any sufficient consolation in providing Being and meaning. But in its way the refusal to forget is an ambiguous argument and can become the imposition of victims who make use of it as an argument for behaving like victors. So the refusal to forget cannot be an unstoppable argument in defense of the Victim. Anamnesis, reparation, the duty to remember [*devoir de memoire*] in general serves both parties in a near reversal and enters into the twisted logic of history. I would like to say that the Victim-in-person does not reverse the institutions of thought nor of law but that she inverts their course or their processes through her radicality.

PP: *If the Victim forces us to think, she does not necessarily move us to philosophize like the "great criminals" do, whether they are or are not part of history, and who can inspire a Sadean or Nietzschean philosopher. The new forms of history, those of social mores, the everyday, marginalities and minorities, of "little events," these cannot replace thinking for the victims.*

FL: The modest, archivist, rightly grey history is small change for the big money that it solicits, but it is always the history of the victors which expresses the order of the World, of the learned over the unlearned, of the bright over the humble, of precisely the intellectuals over the "masses." There is no history of the defeated that we could call "radical," but in every battle there are those who are on this losing side; they do not leave behind grandiose monuments and very few documents, they do not create a system for their forgetting or their remembrance. For the intellectuals to begin to glimpse the problem of the Victim we had to wait, though it was already too late, for the equivocal revolt of Jewish memory, monuments to mass graves and documents concerning "concentration," then the witnesses of the Gulags and those who follow, and still the intellectuals have reconstituted anew some complicity there. Different from the symbol which is suggested [*donne à penser*] in the philosophical distance of interpretation and its traps, the Victim only suggests inasmuch as she forces or determines the play of religious or juridical interpretation (for example the knowledge that produces a judgment or a process) through her own being-given. Even the "judgement of God," which turns towards theodicy, engenders its own victims and must be determined according to the Victim-in-person. As for the "judgment of history," which never stops rendering verdicts precisely in favor of the criminals who establish it, more than others its victims suspend its "conclusions" [*conclusions*] without appeal. The intellectual that the Victim assumes as a subject is not opposed head-on to the judgment (of the victors) of history, in a desperate face-to-face that would immediately return him into an executioner. He appears in the mode of the "in-face" [*en-face*], the unique face that, under the Name-of-the-victim, the intellectual can assume without hiding another more secret side, like a hinter-victim.[1] The Victim-in-person is not the parousia of history and yet she is manifest, unforgettable, and does not stop diffusing her necessary identity throughout history. To put it yet another way, the represented victim causes us to think [*donne à penser*]; the Victim-in-person forces thought or makes us think her [*donne le penser*] as a force without providing the means to think with.

PP: *What, finally, do you criticize the intellectuals for?*

FL: Non-Philosophy makes the effort it does so as to dispel a transcendental appearance proper to the intellectuals and the result of the confusion of the intellectual's identity with distinct types. The illusion of the disengaged intellectual is that he believes in a truth that is itself neoliberal, which consists in describing much more closely the appearances of an operation or an event, in repeating what the politics of capitalism and globalization constantly do, write, and tell, and in embellishing them with moral considerations about the victims. In general this is a confusion of the academic and the intellectual, the latter adding opinion onto opinion. The illusion of the intellectual engaged in the old way, is that he believes, on the contrary, that an *a priori* decision grounded upon some ideology anticipating the meaning of events is able to provide assistance to the victims. In general this is a confusion of the political militant and the intellectual. One searches for the truth and

---

[1] *En-face* literally means "opposite" as in "across the way," but Laruelle is playing on that meaning with his own syntax of the "in" which escapes translation. [Translator's note.]

remains an empiricist and rudderless, the other provides the truth and twists the events all the way to failure. Certain intellectuals claim more and more the status of "citizen," kind of a makeshift solution for one who is engaged–disengaged, ashamed of their former choices, and which reduces their ambitions to being more useful than a traditional academic and more prudent than a militant. Empiricist or *a priori* truth, both in reality ground themselves in history, which plays the role of a "natural attitude," as the phenomenologists called it, legitimating judgments and actions. But can history, and now the situation concerning citizenship, rightly ground and legitimate the practice of the intellectual in a radical, but not idealist, way? Under these three most notable forms, the historical or dominant intellectual produces opinion for opinion, eventually rectifying it, adding to communication, augmenting the flux of news, and making the history-world function. From the point of view of the Victim-in-person, taken here as criterion, the dominant intellectual is in his manner a super victimizing machine.

PP: *Does the antithetical mean anything for you? Doesn't contradiction precisely form the richness of intellectual debate?*

FL: Reason is always in effect divided between extreme and coupled conceptions, more or less connected, both based on the confusion between history and the Name-of-Man. But if I denounce transcendental appearance, which the intellectuals are the victims of, the use made here of certain quasi-Kantian procedures must not cause us to confuse the Victim-in-person and the Victim in-itself (*Ding an sich*). The in-person is so little a thing and so little a thing in itself that the Real which it designates is radically human and certainly not a substance or an Idea. The Idea can be declared "human" but Man-in-person cannot be ideal or an entity of Reason.

PP: *Does this intellectual work for the Victim somewhere?*

FL: The new intellectual is overwhelmed by the urgency of service and intervention – his is an activity of "un-work" [*désoeuvre*] rather than of idleness [*désoeuvrement*]; this activity has lost the meaning of and demand for work like a legacy accumulated and liable to be exploited by its heirs. We recognize the idealist restlessness of the madness that feigns practice through the absence of such works which form a trace of space and time. It may be necessary to compare the intellectuals with the "beautiful soul," their apparent opposite. The confusion here is found in the gulf between this absence of effective work, and, on the other hand, the determined intellectual's character performed-in-the-last-humaneity, the practice of which is instead a non-work distinguished from the "un-work." A non-work is not the absence of work nor the loss of work at its foundation, it is not idleness, nor artistic production, but it is a cloned and determined work, universal rather than "grounded," *any practice or production* [exécution] *with the materials close by.*

But the duality of the intellectual would be meaningless if it amounts to denouncing a transcendental dialectic in the work of the dominant intellectuals, a transcendental dialectic based upon an apparent and confused conception of the Victim's reality. The prac-

tice of the intellectual is only determinate if the kinds
or schemes of action are proposed in other ways,
which are those of the dominant intellectual. Each
time it is a problem to be resolved rather than a typical
framework to be reproduced. The practice consists in
re-employing the dominant techniques of intervention
or assistance concerning concrete victims as variables or
arguments within a function, the constant of which is
the Victim-in-person.

PP: *All of that seems very distant from the major problem centers of our time: Americanism (interventionism
and culture), liberalism, globalization, progressivism,
citizenship, anti-Semitism, humanism, terrorism, mal-
nutrition, exclusion, internal and external security, the
Middle East, Europe, etc.*

FL: The list is vast, of course, where each of us freely
forms their intellectual menu (every blending is permit-
ted), but these combinations are no longer pertinent
from the moment when they are no longer considered to
be universally valid for victims, meaning for all humans
in the grip of the major institutional bodies like History,
Economy, Philosophy, Democracy, the State, etc. But
the determined intellectual can put a lot of work into
each of these problems, which are very real in their
"materiality," and stop treating them like absolutes,
"individuating" them in-the-last-victim. Everything can
be used, even certain lawful protests, even an action of
a revolutionary or insurrectionary kind, provided that
all of this is provided "provisionally" under the ultimatum of the determining Victim. Even certain forms
of terrorism – certainly not all, and the religious kind

even less so as they are based on absolute beliefs – but provided that they do not in turn engender, in a circular manner, other forms of terror.

PP: *What do you think about the mistakes in the intellectuals' assessment? The examples are famous.*

FL: Why is it that intellectuals deceive themselves or are so often contradicted by the course of history? In reality an absurd question, it is history in its constant inconsistency, religious, political, or economic beliefs that deceive us or fail us without any respite and which drag along their followers, those who claim not to dominate them, undoubtedly, but who ideologically dominate victims through their own means and under their own authority. The classic argument against the intellectuals, *that they are immunized against the real*, is only an argument by definition or a tautological argument and so not a very effective one, provided that we understand that strictly speaking they are pro-tected against *reality* – since they defend values that are separated out – or against the Real, since they defend reality. But it is simply less analytic and more critically effective if it is implied [*sous-entend*] that these values would have to vary simply *according to the reality* of victims, and to be invariable as regards that constant, the Victim-in-person. A true critique begins with a func-tionally consistent but not inadequate relation, or rather some consistency of the inadequacy of the variation of reality and the Real. This is only possible if this con-stant or identity of inadequacy is Man-in-person, who determines concrete victims, each time defined under the condition of that constant. The intellectual, witness cloned from victims by the Victim-in-person, is the place where the defended ethical values determine themselves according to the true reality of these victims. The solution which cleanses the intellectual of this critique and objection, all the while partially showing him in his cogency, is the "existent-Stranger" intellectual.

PP: *Doesn't it seem like there is something of the utopian spirit in your position? Wouldn't François Laruelle himself be an extraterrestrial?*

FL: My concepts are sort of like extraterrestrials and I do rub the intellectuals' ideology up the wrong way. The wrong way [*à rebours*], that says it all. For I regret following this classical way, if I end up with considerations concerning the utopia necessary for intellectuals. In reality we should have to begin with utopia or uchronia as the positioning of the problem, but that would hardly be comprehensible and would have seemed to be a useless provocation. However, I hold this not so much to set everything back up that has already come to be said, but to give utopia its true sense which is the uchronia of the Real. I would like to reintroduce the spirit of utopia into the work of the intellectuals, who practice it by measuring the spirit of utopia according to history and dissimulate it through its interstices, through its interworlds. I do not believe in the thesis which would like to substitute imagination for utopia, which as far as I can tell concerns a utopia that is in reality intra-historical and without real force, and so precisely about imagination. But the problem for the intellectual is that of establishing an anti-, or better yet non-, historical (in the sense that I mean in general by "non-") practice of history.

---

PP: *History and utopia, like Cioran.*

FL: Except that I no longer make a simple duality out of history and utopia, a gnostico-religious duality, like those of two worlds. The intellectual only has a single World anyway, this is history, he has to engage with it in one way or another. But there are just two ways of relating to it. The first is based upon the natural belief in history as a determining cause of every position taken [*prise de position*], ground or terrain of every validation. It pulls the war of positions into reflective consideration, these are the conscientious intellectuals, or *into consciousness*, the dominant ones, who unceasingly "take a position," often disguised as "taking a stand" [*prises de parti*] and who simulate this war by producing in their way, as modern strategies, political and ethical scenarios, humanitarian scenarios. In general the second way takes Man-in-person (under the name of Victim-in-person) as a determining cause of an intellectual practice *for* victims as such. The Victim does not reform a world or a history, either because she is the residue or the *remainder* left by the operations which ground the World and history, or because she is a cause, precisely uchronic, of a practice. She is the ground of human immanence that comes from nowhere and from no history in order to affect the intellectual, and therefore one determined as an inversion of the order of consciousness and causality. The Victim merges with what I call "the spirit of struggle" or the void that unilaterally determines practice or forms the presupposed that calls for practice without furnishing it with its means. She announces herself in-person as the future that is radically empty of time and history, presents and pasts, but which has the power to *force* the intellectuals to turn themselves towards the World as all at once constitutive and regulative of the acts of violence [*exactions*] against man. Forcing the intellectuals to take on humans as those injured by history and those humiliated by the World . . .

PP: *By inverting the sense of history?*

FL: Effectively, I no longer consider the Victim as a piece of trash that has to be recycled within the course of normal existence (yes, it is unpleasant but that's how it is) and as something that requires a certain amount of care. Even if she is treated as a therapeutic or a "juridic," I stop treating her as a remainder of philosophy or of history in order to make her the determining cause which provides reality and identity, not for history, but for a theoretical and practical perspective about her. If philosophy has engendered the dominant intellectual, the determined intellectual at the heart of the matter involves a disruption of his function and his object. The Victim inverts, as definitively or structurally future, the course of universal history. She does not reverse it once and for all to continue history in a way that is more rickety than truly chaotic. Reversing and inversing are not the same gesture. To reverse is to rectify an erected idol, history – this is what every philosopher does, especially the most recent ones like Deleuze and Foucault, and even Derrida. But to uni-lateralize is to invert the World, to make history fall from the height of its pretensions to meaning or to some "end." To invert is a radical gesture that can only come from nowhere, meaning from Man-in-person, and which uni-lateralizes history and other forms of domination. This is at bottom how I would summarize the situation: the Victim never stops "overturning" [*ne cesse de faire que "verse"*] that rickety chariot which the philosophers want to prevent from falling over and that they are trying to push back up and put back on the road. Enough of this palliative care and prolonging of life through technical means that is focused upon history. A moribund or sick imaginary, it may be time – no, the future demands – that a usage other than this referential one be made of it in some state of survival or some unduly prolonged paradigm.

PP: *Would one have to turn into a mystic? This is not the first time that the intellectual and the mystic have tried to form an alliance behind the back of the philosopher, but it is rare . . .*

FL: The Victim-in-person, which has no place within the World or in time or in history, but who finds in each of these only "occasions" to come, I would not hesitate to say that she comes from . . . and for . . . these occasions as a specifically human grace. Let me be clear that we are not at all in the Jewish context and not at all in the Christian context. To put it simply, this grace only arrives in actuality as future and is in no way the effect of some transcendence (the Christian God-of-grace or the Jewish Other-God), but is the effect of a unilaterality of that radical immanence which is Man-in-person. We are not in the service of God nor of that of the Other man. The principal objective is not a form of humanitarian aid or assistance, nor an infinite responsibility, but human life insofar as it is possible to determine it through the first name of the Victim. This objective sufficiently determines (but without providing the concrete means, let me repeat that) the others, like that of humanitarian aid. I would not say that this is a mystical vision of the intellectual, even though it makes possible a new usage of the mystic within her own order. It is rather a "heretical" vision (like the one developed in *Future Christ*) and a "messianic" vision or, better still with hopes of limiting in this way certain otherwise inevitable misunderstandings, it is a messianity of the intellectual. By this term I appropriate, generalize, formalize, and extract from the Judeo-Christian context those themes or terms that have their origin in that context but not at all definitive claims [*titulaire définitif*] upon them. I am not confusing the concept's original or originary background and its being positioned in and set to theoretical functions. This confusion is a distant root, one way of working dominant intellectuals.

PP: *They can hardly accept this solution . . .*

FL: The problem isn't whether they accept it or not – at any rate they can only resist it. We will not force them to be free but – maybe this is what remains for us of Rousseau – the victims will force them to be "free from" the history-world, and as for the rest they will "resist." The deepening of crises, the exacerbation of possible types of decision like terrorism or complicity, revolution or globalization, rebellion or consensus, but also the complementary impossibility of making a clear decision, make the position of the intellectuals untenable anyway and somewhat desperate, as they waver between ridicule and being pitiful. The victims should encourage them to be a little more Platonic, though always human, and to search for a principle not superior to *doxa* but stranger to it and therefore determinate for the intellectual decision. I defend a strictly human messianity of the intellectual. Let yourself be determined according to the immanent future and you will be forced to assist human life.

PP: *The non-philosopher doesn't fight for the Real. But he does fight for actual reality* [réalité effective] – *this is the paradox – in the name of the Real. He doesn't fight for the Real because, I suppose, he does not have to conquer it. Philosophy believes that conquering the Real is necessary, hence the ever greater, ever stronger, heroism which animates it. The non-philosopher parts with a certain Real, limited elsewhere by virtue of its immanence, and so not supporting philosophical ambition or desire. We have come full circle. I will let you conclude.*

FL: As I often say, the Real is not a problem. What becomes a problem under another form is the relation of the Real to the actual reality of history. It is such that, as soon as we think or do something, we are, through it, thrown into actual reality, turned towards the World but just not imprisoned within the World. The problem is one of utilizing, a second time, a discourse according to the Name-of-Man and no longer the history-world, a discourse whose logic is grounded upon sufficiency and pretension, as well as upon desire. This is a discourse which will be reworked not in its discursive conditions but at the level of the component that determines in-the-last-humaneity – that is, transforms – this discursivity. In the way I would love to see him function too, the intellectual will be limited to his own desire. He will give up the *jouissance* of these false reals, to the foundations of any appearance or imaginary of memory, of the world, of history.

A little like the way in which Levinas says that the Other person [*Autrui*] is goodness itself, I would say that the Victim is peace-in-person. She comes, a Future, to affect history and its background noise, the incessant noise of battle. This is the ultimatum of peace. It is not pacifism, it is not ethics (the transcendence of the Other person), the Victim is not the straw man of God. This is the future, a unilaterality, towards which Man forces history. I have nothing more on my mind [*à penser*] beyond these formulas . . . I believe I have said enough. No, just one more word, there were no examples here, non-philosophy is a practice, it is enacted [*en acte*], almost criminally performative [*performative au crime près*], this is the only way of demonstrating it. For the rest, please refer to your daily newspaper.

PP: *I certainly will.*

# *Index*

# Index

ideology 41, 55, 84, 95, 138
immanence 31, 38, 50, 52, 64,
    89, 91, 94, 121, 144
    and Man 100
    radical 44, 146
    of World 104
inequality 74
intellectuals 1, 3, 16, 35
    function/role 2–3, 6
"Intellectuals and Power" 55
Iraq 63
    American intervention
        in 26
Israel 77–8

Jewish people 133, 136, 146
Judaism 78, 85–6, 91
Judeo-Christianity 147
Just, the 90
just war 10, 20, 23
justice 33, 54, 55, 70, 74,
    79–80, 90, 108, 125, 132,
    133–4, 135

*kairos* 129, 130
kamikaze 75
Kant, Immanuel 20, 33, 36, 96,
    105, 121, 125, 139–40
Kierkegaard, Søren 87
knowing 40

Lacan, Jacques 26, 29, 30, 41,
    45, 46, 47, 52,
    117, 118
"laid-out Victim" 75
language 31, 32, 41–2, 46–7,
    49, 65, 74, 94, 104, 112,
    117, 122–3
    games 38
Laruelle, François 2
"learned ignorance" 40
left-wing intellectuals 6
Leibniz, G. W. F. 60
Lenin, V. I. 57
    Levi, Primo 24, 34, 78

Levinas, Emmanuel 21, 103,
    131, 149, 131, 149
Lévy, Bernard-Henri 17

Man 23, 31, 82–3, 92, 94, 95,
    100, 118, 125, 128
Man-in-Man 38, 45, 91, 119,
    129, 142
Man-in-person 23, 24, 26,
    28, 31, 35, 36, 37, 38–9,
    43, 47, 49, 51, 62, 65, 66,
    70–1, 83, 90, 95, 103, 113,
    123, 124, 131, 140, 144
    and history 126
    philosophizability 43–4
    as presupposed 97
Manichaeism 84–5
Marx 45, 47, 59, 85
Marxism 84–5, 90, 110,
    120
Marxists 10, 57, 85, 118
mathematical physics 21
media practices 18, 59, 128
mediation 54, 68, 76
mediatization 54, 59, 68
Messiah 119
messianity 127, 147–8
metaphysics 21
Milner, Jean-Claude 19–20
morality 84–5
mystic 146, 147

Name-of-Man *see* Man-in-
    person
Name-of-the-victim 137–8
Nazism 13
New-Born 48, 49, 65
Nietsche, Friedrich Wilhelm 13,
    18–19, 21, 24, 32, 33,
    42–3, 56–7, 58, 80, 92, 96,
    98, 104, 118, 121, 136
*Nietzsche contra
    Heidegger* 56–7
non-analysis 41
*non-engaged* intellectual 10

---

153

# Index